C000120201

The Art of Interesting

BOOKS OF

FRANCIS P. DONNELLY, S.J.

———

WATCHING AN HOUR

THE HOLY HOUR IN GETHSEMANE

THE HEART OF THE GOSPEL

THE HEART OF REVELATION

MUSTARD SEED

CHAFF AND WHEAT

SHEPHERD MY THOUGHTS (*Verses*)

THE ART OF INTERESTING

THE
ART OF INTERESTING

ITS THEORY AND PRACTICE
FOR
SPEAKERS AND WRITERS

BY

FRANCIS P. DONNELLY, S.J.

UNIV. OF
CALIFORNIA

NEW YORK
P. J. KENEDY & SONS
1921

COPYRIGHT·1920
BY P. J. KENEDY & SONS
PRINTED IN U·S·A

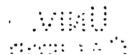

PREFACE

TO be able to arrest and hold the attention of other minds is a useful and necessary power for all speakers and writers. Minds are fickle; minds are wearied or indifferent, and the writer, and especially the speaker, who would propose his truths to the mind for understanding and his motives to the will for action will make a dismal failure if he cannot arrest and hold the attention of audience or readers.

To be clear, to be forceful, these are indeed necessary qualities of expression, but a preliminary condition to clearness and force is interest which will awaken attention and keep attention while the mind is instructed and the will aroused to action. It is that necessary quality of interest which is studied in detail in this book.

The problem which offers difficulty to the advertiser is the same that offers greater difficulty to writer or speaker. The advertiser may make use of pictures and colors and devices of print for the eyes and has usually but a brief, simple message to convey. The

437470

writer, however, has only language, the written and the spoken word, with which he must deliver long, complicated statements to distracted and indifferent minds.

What is useful and what is good win interest by their substance, because the useful and good of their own nature gratify some appetite. It is not such interest this book discusses nor that voluntary interest from sheer force of the will which centers upon a thing despite all contrary feelings of attraction or repulsion. The interest here treated is that which attracts and fascinates by the very form the expression and thought assume in language. The novel, the humorous, the beautiful are in general the qualities which attract the mind.

If we except what are called figures of language as distinguished from figures of thought (cf. Chap. II) and if we set aside certain forms of wit which are mainly verbal, the faculty of the imagination will be found to be the rich source of what is novel, humorous and beautiful. It is therefore the imagination which is the chief topic of the following chapters. "The Place of Imagination in Prose" would serve as a substitute title of the book. In the earlier chapters various, specific manifestations of the imagination are described and exemplified; then follow sev-

eral chapters on particular authors, whose
methods of interesting are examined in detail. The final chapters go into the theory
of imagination, warning against excesses, ex-
plicitly defining ideas and presenting exercises
for developing the faculty of imagination.

To interest by language is a function of the
highest importance and a discussion of the art
of interesting cannot fail to be useful to all
writers and speakers. Literary critics too
will profit by the principles here set forth,
principles based upon a well established philosophy and tested by the experience of ages.
Teachers will find here a solid theory of
rhetorical style, which will be of service to
them in their work. The philosophy of
rhetoric explained and illustrated throughout
the book is the basis of the author's works
on composition, *Model English,* Books I and
II (Allyn and Bacon), which furnish numerous illustrations and practical exercises in the
art of interesting.

The author wishes to thank the editors of
the *Ecclesiastical Review, Catholic World*
and *America* for kind permission to use some
of the chapters appearing first in their
columns.

CONTENTS

	PAGE
THE TIRESOME SPEAKER . . .	3
INTEREST FROM DIRECTNESS . .	19
THE ART OF ELOQUENCE AND THE SCIENCE OF THEOLOGY. . .	37
THE IMAGINATION OF THE SPEAKER	53
INTEREST FROM EMOTIONS. . .	73
MEMORY AS A TEST OF INTEREST	87
NEWMAN AND THE ACADEMIC STYLE	99
PARDOW AND THE POPULAR STYLE	123
INTEREST FROM ANTAGONISM . .	143
MACAULAY AND "JOURNALESE" .	155
LITERARY AGILITY	165
TABB AND FANCY	175
POETRY AND INTEREST. . . .	191
NOVELTY OR ECCENTRICITY . .	199
THE NEED OF IMAGINATION . .	215
DEVELOPING THE IMAGINATION .	225
IS ESTHETIC EMOTION A SPINAL THRILL ?	237
ORIGINALITY BY IMITATION . .	251
EXERCISES FOR THE IMAGINATION	267
SYNOPSIS OF CONTENTS . . .	311

ix

I

THE TIRESOME SPEAKER

THE ART OF
INTERESTING

I

THE TIRESOME SPEAKER

AN amusing outcome of the rivalry and
competition in contemporary business is
the great attention paid to the wrapper.
When we went shopping years ago, our merchants separated our order from the bulk
which he had, put our purchase up in a paper,
and we went home with all our packages done
up in very nearly the same way. Now all
this is changed; everything is handed to us
already done up. The box has as a result
become almost more important than its contents, and advertising campaigns are furi-
ously waged over some new receptacle.
Jellies in automatic jars and candies in convenient cans and biscuits in the best boxes and
pigs'-feet in prize packages; about these
things do the advertisers rage. They are wise

3

men, these modern merchants, and the keen-
ness of competition has led them to discover
a truth which the teachers of rhetoric have
insisted upon from time immemorial. *Non
nova sed nove* is the way they put it, or
translated into business parlance, it would
read, " You had better change the wrapper
if you wish to sell your goods."

The Tiresome Sermon still handles its
merchandise in the bulk, and still uses the
old brown paper and the old ball of cord.
Conventionality and triteness are the chief
factors in producing sermons tiresome in
thought. They are the uninviting receptacles
of old ideas. Unhappily the competition in
the pulpits is not always keen enough to force
an improvement in the package. " We
couldn't beat the contents so we beautified
the box," is the catchword of advertisements,
which might well be applied to the eternal
truths of faith.

It is so much easier to say things in the
same old way. Nobody is disturbed; neither
the slumberers in the pews nor the conventional critics among our clerical friends.
The dignity of the pulpit is not lowered; in
fact the preacher is so far away from his
audience and so high above them that by no
conceivable effort could he come down.
Have a conventional introduction which may

lead anywhere; have conventional divisions; have conventional proofs in a conventional order with conventional conclusions and put your audience in a conventional heaven with a conventional blessing, and conventional critics will give you a conventional criticism and you will be decorous, dignified, and successfully — dull. Omit any of these conventionalities; give something new, fresh, and thought-provoking, but difficult to classify, not conforming to cut-and-dried notions, and you will likely be looked upon as undecorus, undignified to the critics, and very interesting to the congregation.

Words are ever growing old. When first uttered, they are revealers; they hold the mirror up to nature and reflect the object clearly and distinctly. After a time they cease to reveal; they become signs, and then lastly mere symbols. Language begins in poetry and ends in algebraic symbols. Someone has called language fossil poetry. The word candor once meant something shining white, the sun-light of the soul; horror was having the hair stand on end; emolument once gave a picture of the mill and the ground wheat. Who sees those pictures now? Yet once the words were mirrors. Tribunal was the place where sat the officer of the tribe and the word in its early days was a re-

vealer of that seat.   Tribunal afterward de-
noted the place where any judge or officer sat,
and then it became generic and was a sign.
Tribunal as used nowadays in the trite phrase,
" tribunal of penance," has become a mere
colorless symbol for the confessional.   It is
used by the speaker when he is tired saying
confessional; but it may be safely said that
few preachers and fewer hearers see anything else in the term than a mere substitute
for confessional.   Brown paper was once no
doubt a tremendous advance over more primi-
tive methods of handling goods, and tribunal
too once had a revelation.   Put the same
idea now in a new wrapper, as you cannot im-
prove the contents; speak of the court-room
in the church corner, or of the prisoner soul
at the bar, or of the trial where judge and
jury are one and criminal and witness are
one; or in some other way bring back the
word tribunal to its original function of revealing; do that and you will not be trite.
You may send a shudder through the sensitive
organism of conventionality, but you will
make your listeners see visions and dream
dreams — not an insignificant result if we
may believe St. Peter's first sermon.

• As with words, so with illustrations, the
Tiresome Sermon is conventional and trite.
The similes are family heirlooms and are

brought out and dusted as well as possible for use on solemn occasions. They do not meet the thoughts of the listeners. They are not contemporaneous, actual and living. Nothing could be more contemporaneous in thought and expression than the Gospels. Fishermen and shepherds and farmers are spoken to in a language they understand and feel. The vineyard and its vines, the sower and his seed, the fisherman drawing in his net, the harvester and his harvest, the well, the candle, the coin — these constitute the vocabulary of the Gospel sermons and they made up the stock ideas in the mind of the listeners. Everything was fresh and new because it grew out of the life they were living. In fact the talk of the Gospel was often a commentary on an actual event before the eyes of the speaker.

It is interesting to contrast the illustrations in the Gospel with the illustrations in the Epistles of St. Paul. The Epistles are full of running and wrestling and battling. For St. Paul the Christian life was not on the farm but in the city, and his language changed accordingly. If he speaks of the sea, he has the Mediterranean in his imagination, because his hearers had, and not the sea of Galilee. He speaks of being tossed about by the wind of doctrine, and of the anchor of

hope, not of fruitless fishing or breaking nets.
Neither the Gospels nor the Epistles are conventional and trite, for the very good reason
that they used a language understood by the
audience.   The tiresome speaker will use the
same illustration for every audience and for
all time.   Christ likened Himself to a ladder
upon and down which the angels traveled;
conventionality objects to comparing Him to
a locomotive.   Christ called Himself a lamp;
conventionality shudders at an electric light.
Cast spears, shoot arrows in sermons; but do
not discharge rifles.   Quote the leaven, but
avoid saying it is yeast.   The Gospel may
use the processes of digestion to enforce a
truth, but squeamishness would wince at a
reference to the process of breathing or the
circulation of the blood.

Much tiresome preaching is defended on
the plea of dignity.   The preacher must be
dignified, it is constantly said.   Undoubtedly.   But what is undignified?   Is it inde-
corous to speak of washing dishes, mending
clothes, fertilizing [1] fig trees, mixing bread,
feeding pigs?   Yet of these the Gospels
speak.   The answer to this objection is that
if the people understand the thought, and
the illustration hurries them to the thought
instead of halting them on the expression,

---

[1] It is not dignified to quote exactly.

and if the speaker is earnest, and is speaking not to raise a laugh but to vivify an idea, then there is no lack of dignity or danger of it. A few critics may be horrified at an illustration, which their powers of reflection enable them to dissect coldly and heartlessly; a thousand hearers, who have seized a live thought in a live way, will be edified. It might be said too that there are worse things in preaching than a lack of dignity; and one thing which suggests itself for honorable mention is slumberous triteness. To maltreat the words of Tennyson, we may be permitted to remark, the " faultily faultless " can be splendidly dull. St. Augustine assures us: " Melius est ut nos reprehendant grammatici quam ut non intelligant populi." " Better be reproved by the grammarians than not understood by the people."

A French writer has devised a method of never failing in dignity, and it is simplicity itself: never use the specific term, but always the generic. Stop after saying, " Resist not evil "; or, if you will continue, do not use the language of the Gospel. Say not, " If any man strike thee on the right cheek, turn to him the other "; say rather, " If any injury is done to thy person, do not indulge in retaliation." Do not say, " Why seest thou a mote in thy brother's eye; but the beam in thy

own eye thou considerest not?" No!
Have recourse to the French recipe for dignity; say, " To wish to correct our neighbor's
trifling defects, while we neglect our own
vices, is foolish." If you have to deliver a
sermon on scandal, urge the folly of permit-
ting power or activity or knowledge to lead
one into sin and so to incur God's severe
retribution. Thus you will be dignified. Be
specific and you will say with Christ: " And
if·thy hand scandalize thee, cut it off; for it is
better for thee to enter in life maimed, than
having two hands to go into hell, into unquenchable fire."

There are indeed occasions when a translation into the generic is useful. It is useful in
commentary, when we wish to show the general principle involved in a text. It is useful
too where the specific term might suggest
thoughts not in keeping with the idea to be
conveyed or where the specific term would
be so startling as to center attention upon itself. It is bad art or at least not the best of
art to distract the mind from the end to the
means. That would be to lose the picture in
the color, or worse still, in the frame. The
generic again is often suggestive and so helpful. But any continuous avoidance of the
specific terms is bound to result in dull generalities which by their abstraction and intellec-

tual character make an undue and wearisome appeal to the mind and never give the refreshing relief that the species or individual affords to the imagination of the hearers. The sermon, then, that would avoid tiresomeness should always have recourse to the specific and individual. Instead of taking the life and emotion out of the Gospel by transmitting it into the generic and abstract, it should rather translate one specific term into another, as St. Paul did when the audience did not respond to the language appropriate to Palestine. Do not translate the Prodigal Son into the supreme folly of yielding to the spirit of independence, of sacrificing assured comforts and domestic felicity for the glare and glitter of the city, and of being reduced to the extreme straits of penury and to the tardy, though consoling, fruits of penance and forgiveness and mercy. You will be more certain of avoiding tiresomeness if you will do as the late Fr. Van Rensalaer did once in Boston. He told to the men the story of a Boston Prodigal, sobering up in New York and looking up Fr. Van Rensalaer for carfare to take him home. The sermon was not tiresome and no doubt many who heard the preacher then could tell you that parable today.

The subject of parables leads to the dis-

cussion of another method of avoiding tiresomeness.   The spoken word which is heard
once and must make its impression whilst
echoing in the listeners' ears, will necessarily
be more diffuse than writing or print which
can be repeatedly consulted.   That is one
reason, no doubt, why parables abound in the
Gospels and are absent from the Epistles.
Many of the splendid comparisons of St.
Paul would have been amplified, we may be
sure, to the length and vividness of a parable
if they had been spoken.   The people like a
play, and the preacher who can stage his
thoughts in the imagination of his hearers
may be sure of a delighted audience.   The
comparison as a story is interesting; the parable made into a drama is thrilling.   No one
need go outside the Gospel to learn the art
of dramatizing thought, an indispensable
requisite for one who would successfully escape tiresomeness.   The thought must be
deeply entered into; the mind must go down
to the details of the thought for the background and incidents and characters of his
Sunday morning mystery play.   Under that
scrutiny and meditation the suggestive detail
will stand out, the characters will be distinctly
etched, and the thrilling scenes will come to
the surface of consciousness.   How tame the
panegyric of St. John the Baptist might have

become! How vivid and direct and significant it is in the dramatic dialogue where by interested questions and imagined answers Christ brought out in suggestive pictures and growing dignity the grandeur of the Baptist, the desert, the reed, the fine garments, Elias! Every one of the Gospel parables partakes of this dramatic power to some extent, and the simple experiment of telling the story without dialogue and vivid detail will disclose another way, if one were needed, of becoming tiresome. It might be well, however, to mention here that parable of the rich man whose land brought forth plenty of fruits. In the first act the successful farmer soliloquizes with his soul and determines to build increased storage room for his larger crops; in the second act he contentedly lays out a program for a long life of plenty and cheer; in the third act comes the doom of God with tragic swiftness: " Thou fool! "

It will have been noticed that tiresome sermons are found where imagination is lacking. Who is it that touches up in brighter colors the faded and worn words and gives them back, where possible, their original splendor? It is the one who does not make a practice of using words as mere symbols. The philosophic mind, when soaring among rarified abstractions, is hampered by any distracting collision with concreteness. The philosopher must be metaphysical, and the imagination is physical. It will not be put off with pale abstractions or faded pictures. It always keeps the reality in view when it has recourse to a verbal substitute for the reality. It sees things when it thinks and is ever impatient with words that do not reveal.

It is the imagination too that in consequence is actual and specific. It cannot be anything else. Its brightest visions are those of memory; and when it would revivify, it becomes contemporaneous and actual, moving among the pictures which grace its walls and have the added interest of being its own composition. Partial to its work, the imagination points out the appropriate scenes to fill the generic frames of the mind when that generalizing faculty utters a wide truth. "Give," said Christ, "and it will be given unto you." Then the artist imagination comes with its picture: "Good measure, pressed down and shaken together and running over." "Take heed that you do not your justice before men"; so speaks the intellect. "Therefore when thou doest an almsdeed sound not a trumpet before thee," so speaks the imagination. It is, in fact, characteristic of all good thinking to follow up the general truth, satisfactory to the mind, with its particular instance which shall please and delight the heart and emotions.

It is the imagination finally which must expand comparisons into parables and parables into brief plays. The priest's training in philosophy and theology has perhaps made him timid about the word "imagination." He thinks of poetry and fairy-tales and fiction and that sparkle and foam which will amuse us when on life's vacation by the sea-shore. If that were all there is to imagination, then none of it should be in sermons. Poetry is not for the pulpit. The soul that is famishing must have something better than husks; it cries for a fatted calf. The same faculty, however, will furnish both, the dainty beauty of poetry and the solid flesh, red with blood, provided by the oratorical imagination. That faculty then stages the vigorous thought of the mind, manages the entrances and exits, acts as costumer and director, bringing some characters to the front of the stage and grouping others in the background, keeping all in activity with dialogue and monologue and changing scenes and alternating interest and suspense and climax and dénouement. The imagination is the natural enemy of Tiresome Sermons.

II

INTEREST FROM DIRECTNESS

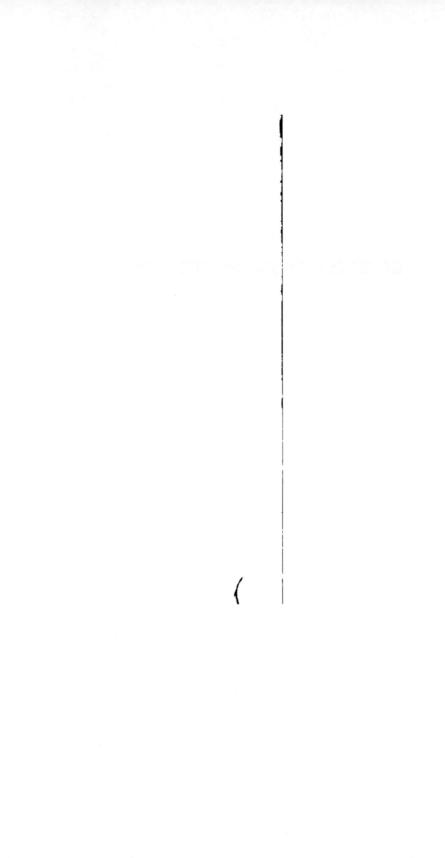

II

INTEREST FROM DIRECTNESS

A FRENCH writer has defined eloquence as the art of saying something to some one. That is directness. A sermon is talked; it has a definite subject and a definite audience. A tiresome sermon is often such because it is addressed to no one in particular and because it is writing, not speaking, although it may be delivered without paper or book. Many tiresome sermons are things read from the tablets of the memory. They are essays, not talks. They have the whole world for an audience, not any particular part of it. Unless one speaks extempore — and there is some hesitation about advising that course — there is every likelihood that the written sermon will not often rise out of the style of print. It is somewhat incongruous to talk to a sheet of paper through a fountain-pen or a typewriter. The writer of a sermon may begin with, " my dear brethren," but that is the only sign that he is talking to any one. The audience disappears from his sight in the process of the composi-

19

tion, and he is so engrossed in the work of formulating his thoughts in his mind and casting them into suitable expression that there is no attempt made or no energy left to direct the composition toward living ears rather than project it upon dead paper.

Strange, too, as it may seem, the more care is given to a sermon, the more likely is it to become an essay. The preacher himself may have in view a volume of sermons, or the occasion, which has called for more careful composition, will likely be one that will be honored with an account in the press. In either case the sermon is written for the eye, rather than for the ear, to be read rather than to be heard. The audience is not a definite one, but the whole world. Instead of saying something to some one, the speaker writes something — more usually anything — to anyone.

What is the effect upon a speech of an audience, either actually present or distinctly imagined? Fortunately it is not hard to realize. Read the *Congressional Record* containing the speeches given in regular debate and the issues given up to the reproduction of memorial discourses. The debates, especially in those parts where the speaker is interrupted or likely to be, are vigorous, direct, lively; whereas the memorials are wearisome biographical essays, vapid, exaggerated, even bombastic, and containing tasteless flowers of speech which would shrivel in the faintest heat of conflict. It is true indeed that panegyric belongs to a different type of oratory from debate and cannot be as direct. So much the better for our present purpose. The contrast in Congress may well illustrate the difference between a talk in the pulpit and a chapter of a book read, or as good as read, in the same place.

Demosthenes has always been pointed to as more direct than Cicero. Cicero has more commonplaces, more frequent digressions to the general truth, the particular application of which is under discussion. The difference, we believe, will be found due in a large part to the audience. Demosthenes spoke before the people in the Athenian assembly, with the opposition watching intently every word. Demosthenes felt their presence and stripped himself of the luxuriance of style. " There is Phocion," he said, " the pruner of my periods." Cicero, on the other hand, spoke most frequently in the senate, or if he spoke in the court, he was usually chosen to sum up the case and make the emotional appeal, because of his power in moving juries. Is it not worthy too of note that Cicero wrote books and no doubt looked

toward publication, whereas Demosthenes
has left us only speeches? A like contrast,
illustrating the same difference between the
essay and the speech, between dissertations
and debates, between writers and speakers, is
found in Burke and Fox. Burke was called
the dinner-bell of the house of Commons.
He was writing books, composing philosophy
and emptying the benches, while Fox spoke
far into the night and even to the next morning and prodded tired members into constant
attention. A few years ago the present
writer had an experience which showed the
difference between talking and, what might
be called, discoursing. One of the most eloquent orators of our time was addressing an
audience in Faneuil Hall, Boston. His
speech was frequently interrupted with cheers
and applause. When, however, the speaker
was somewhat advanced in his topic, he entered upon a digression, consisting of lengthy
descriptions of an event not directly connected with the subject of the meeting. The
people who a minute or two before had been
applauding, began to rise and leave the hall.
The orator finally noted the exodus, dropped
his historical essay, went back to his talk and
kept his audience attentive and enthusiastic
to the end. An editor recently declared:
" The old style of declamatory speech died a

natural death.   Its revival would be inconsistent with the spirit of the age; it would
savor of an anachronism; our best speakers
have a colloquial manner.   But they are too
few." This voices the modern demand for
talks rather than for disquisitions.

A better way still to appreciate the effect
of saying something to someone rather than
of composing for the wide, wide world, is
found in letters, letters, be it understood,
which are real letters, not masquerading as
such because of an initial " Dear Sir."   In a
letter the audience is a definite individual to
whom everything is addressed with a directness that is scarcely possible even in the best
speeches.   Imagine a letter-writer forgetting
the one he addresses and delivering himself
of learned discourses.   It would be easier to
imagine a man transmitting over a telephone
a chapter of Burke's *On the Sublime and
Beautiful.*   How the thought in a letter is
pointed and epigrammatic, how it discards
useless digressions and delivers itself of no
ponderous platitudes, how free it is from all
pretence at fine writing or elaborate theorizing! How the sentences are light-footed, running on as a rule, but stopping now and then
to allow the insertion of a passing remark,
never stiffening into the self-conscious firmness which would come upon them if they

felt they were to make their debut in print, nor dragging heavily along under the weight of some philosophical profundity. But you will say letters are trivial and chatty and deal with a series of unconnected facts and are for one individual, while sermons are quite the contrary. True enough! Nor is it intended to assert that letters are sermons. Yet letters do however illustrate the effect of an audience upon composition, and that fact would be sufficient reason for mentioning them in this connexion.

Fortunately, however, we can go farther with the illustration. We have in existence and at hand letters on serious and sacred subjects, treating of the highest truths of faith, letters addressed to a whole congregation, having all the spontaneity, freshness, and directness of that style of composition without their ephemeral and trivial character. These letters are the Epistles of St. Paul; letters which are true sermons. St. Augustine in the fourth book of his *Doctrina Christiana,* which may be well styled the first Christian rhetoric, has enthusiastic studies in St. Paul's eloquence. The great Doctor of the Church, who had himself been a teacher of rhetoric, takes no exaggerated view of rhetorical precepts. " Often," he says, " do we find speakers without precepts surpassing those who have mastered them, but no one has ever been eloquent without hearing or reading speeches." He advocates, in consequence, the reading and imitation of Scripture and says, " I could, did leisure permit, point out in the Sacred Scriptures all the good qualities and beauties of eloquence."

He declares too that the reader while engrossed with the sense of the sacred text will insensibly be saturated with the style. To enforce his teaching on the use of Scripture for preachers, he does not disdain to subject an eloquent passage of St. Paul to close analysis, pointing out in detail how clauses and phrases vary in number and length and nature, how statements are mingled with questions or interrupted with parentheses, which we may call the foot-notes of the spoken word. The passage thus analyzed is II Cor. 11 : 16–30, and surely there cannot be found anywhere anything less tiresome, anything more direct, more unlike a dogmatical disquisition and yet anything better fitted to convey the truths of faith with definiteness of audience and liveliness of the spoken word.

An essay is written for the eye; a sermon is spoken for the ear and is profoundly influenced by the consciousness in the speaker of addressing an audience rather than of printing his thoughts for the world in general.

An eye looking into your eye, an ear heeding
your every word, a mind to be affected now
or never, these key a man up, make his
thoughts brisk and energetic and promote
greater efforts to be clear and direct.   There
is all the difference between composing a sermon for readers and composing for listeners
that there is between working by the day or
working by contract, between laboring alone
and under the eye of a master.   The fertile
distinction between essay and talk deals a
hard blow to tiresome sermons and the distinction has not yet exhausted its possibilities.
In the spoken word there is an animation
that seems out of place in an essay.   There
are indeed essays which are talks just as
there are talks that are essays.   Lamb's
chatty, vivacious essays are really bits of
earnest conversation.   Such essays, however,
are exceptions.   To write conversations
looks like pretence or artificiality.   What is
natural and inevitable in conversation seems
forced and out of place when writing-paper
takes the place of a companion.   So the
whole style of sermons when they are written, is likely to doff all the animation of conversation.

What are all the so-called figures of words
but the traits of the spoken words classified
and ticketed with technical names?   A re-

cent writer on rhetoric has no difficulty in showing by a cleverly imagined scene that all the figures of speech are daily occurring around us. It would, no doubt, surprise many, as it surprised Molière's Upstart to learn he was speaking prose, to learn that they are indulging every day in such tremendous things as *conversion, complexion, conduplication, asyndeton* or *dissolution, polysyndeton, anticipation, correction, doubt, communication, apostrophe, hypotyposis* and *aposiopesis.* The list would send an ordinary man to the nearest doctor. Yet what do all these terms do but formulate in scientific language the differences between what is written and what is spoken? In the light of this truth, is it remarkable to learn that St. Paul abounds in these so-called figures of speech? Some will have it he must have derived all his rhetoric from Greek scholars in Tarsus. However that may be St. Paul's Epistles furnish us with endless examples of the most ornate figures of speech. The strict climax, a combination of repetition of the preceding thought with the ordinary climax, is rare enough in literature, because its artifice is too evident. Cicero has but few examples and Demosthenes still fewer, while St. Paul has, besides others elsewhere, three examples in Romans. " We glory also in tribulations, knowing that tribulation worketh patience, and patience trial, and trial hope, and hope confoundeth not." [1] Oxymoron, a seeming contradiction in terms, is another figure in which art is apparent. It is frequently found in the poets and not uncommon among the orators. It is a favorite beauty with St. Paul and takes no small part in imparting vivacity to his style. A beautiful example occurs in the middle of the eloquent sixth chapter of the II Corinthians. " As deceivers, and yet true; as unknown, and yet known; as dying and behold we live; as chastised and not killed; as sorrowful and yet always rejoicing; as needy, yet enriching many; as having nothing, and possessing all things." Paronomasia, or play on words, is St. Paul's quite frequent figure. This is surely a most remarkable fact that St. Paul should play on words, should indulge in what are really puns, although serious ones. Most of these, of course, are lost to us in the English translation. Twenty-one instances are cited by authorities. The famous example of paronomasia in Demosthenes' Speech on the Crown, 11, is almost duplicated in Romans, 12: 3. Demosthenes says, " With all your guile, Aschines, you were so guileless as to be beguiled into think-

[1] Rom. 5:3; cf. 8:29; 10:14.

ing," etc., while St. Paul is rendered thus by Farrar: "Not to be high-minded above what we ought to be minded but to be minded so as to be sober-minded." St. Paul plays too on the name of Onesimus, profitable. "I beseech thee for my son whom I have begotten in my bands, Onesimus, who hath been heretofore unprofitable to thee, but now is profitable both to thee and to me."

Attention has been called to these more striking figures to show how St. Paul made his language almost strain itself in an effort to be varied and interesting and to avoid tedious monotony. It is unnecessary to mention instances of the more usual figures which abound in every letter of St. Paul. Even in the use of ordinary figures such as repetition he strives for point. The well-known passage, "one Lord, one faith, one baptism," is still more striking in the original Greek, where "one" is carried through the three genders of the nominative case. Thirty different kinds of figures in all are pointed out by Farrar. It is to these figures we may ascribe the extraordinary energy of St. Paul's style, an energy which made St. Jerome say: "As often as I read him, I seem to hear not words but the rolling of thunder. They appear to be the words of a simple and guileless rustic; of one who could not lay snares nor escape them; yet look where you will they are lightning flashes. He is persistent in his attempt; he captures anything he attacks; he retreats in order to be victorious; he feigns flight in order the better to slay his foe."

The sacred essay of the pulpit lacks point because its audience is vaguely visualized; lacks life because it shuns the emphasis of a lively style, which looms too prominently in print. Figures have an artificial sound to nimble critics who can in their thoughts outstrip the speaker and, while they are waiting for him to catch up, can leisurely and coldly dissect his language. Figures have an artificial look on the written page where the eye can see a dozen repetitions at a glance or reread a passage until its art is manifest. But the inexperienced ear has not the power of the cold critic or the wide-reaching eye. It takes in one thing at a time; it does not anticipate and with difficulty reflects. Impression must be had upon it while the words are setting its auditory nerves tingling. If the style is direct and vigorous, the ear does not analyze. It is too busy with the thought and does not, like critic or reader, separate the thought from the expression.

As the true listener is more simple and unreflecting, the true speaker is more likely to be expansive and emotional. Emotion shrinks away abashed from the written page. There are indeed earnest essays couched in burning words. As a rule, however, essays are predominantly intellectual and not emotional. They aim at conveying the truth clearly, not at steeping it in fire and fervor that it may touch the heart. I should be very glad to have every reader thrill with the conviction that it is necessary to talk and not to deliver essays in the pulpit; but I hesitate to enforce the lesson with the intense emotional appeal that one would naturally use before an audience. I fear the cold print; I dread the inflexibility of reason. Logic chills the heart. The truth is so insistent that it be put fully and clearly and orderly with division and subdivision and rigid proofs and irrefutable conclusions, that emotion never has a chance at all. Dogmatic disquisitions take the place of sermons. A thesis is put into an essay and another tiresome half-hour is the result.

Say something to someone. If a few sparks of the fire which rages sometimes in conversation, were thrown into a thesis, trying to masquerade as a sermon, there would be less tiresomeness in the pulpit. The essay is dull because it never flames into feeling. Here again St. Paul's Epistles will be

the best school for unlearning tiresomeness.
His great heart beats volcanic at the depths
of his thought and his style heaves irregu-
larly, tossed and broken by the pent-up heat
and force.   He cries out and vehemently
protests.   He lifts his voice in fear; he ten-
derly entreats; he is shocked; he is horrified;
he is aglow with love and aflame with anger.
Never can such emotion be tiresome.   Mark
the feeling surging to the surface in the elev-
enth chapter of the Second Epistle to the
Corinthians: "Would to God that you
could bear with some little of my folly: but
do bear with me.   For I am jealous of you
with the jealousy of God. . . . Although I
be rude in speech, yet not in knowledge.   Or
did I commit a fault, humbling myself that
you might be exalted?   Because I preached
unto you the Gospel of God freely? . . .
The truth of Christ is in me that this glory-
ing shall not be broken off in me in the regions of Achaia.   Wherefore?   Because I
love you not?   God knoweth it . . I say
again, (let no man think me to be foolish,
otherwise take me as one foolish, that I also
may glory a little). . . . I speak according
to dishonor, as if we had been weak in this
part.   Wherein if any man dare (I speak
foolishly). I dare also. They are Hebrews? So am I. They are Israelites?

So am I.   They are the seed of Abraham?
So am I.   They are the ministers of Christ?
(I speak as one less wise.)   I am more.   In
many more labors, in prisons more frequently, in stripes above measure, in deaths
often.   Of the Jews five times did I receive
forty stripes save one."   And then, after a
triumphant recounting of details, " Who is
weak and I am not weak? Who is scandal-
ized and I am not on fire? . . . The God
and Father of our Lord Jesus Christ, who is
blessed forever, knoweth that I lie not."

What would become of the tiresome sermon if it felt the earthquake shock of such
talking and such stormy emotion?   Even the
elocution would immensely profit by this
process.   No one uses preachers' tones in
conversation, and if the style of our sermons
had the directness of a letter and the traits
of talk which rhetoricians call figures, and
above all if those sermons melted their logic
in the lava of feeling, all of which St. Paul
does, the sermon would cease to be an essay
and would to a large extent cease to be tiresome.

III

THE ART OF ELOQUENCE AND THE SCIENCE OF THEOLOGY

III

THE ART OF ELOQUENCE AND THE SCIENCE OF THEOLOGY

THE antithesis of science and art has been so often formulated that it would be idle and wearisome to rehearse the details. Without entering, then, upon the larger question of the contrasts of art and science, it might be well to single out some difficulties the speaker may be expected to meet with in transmuting the substance of his theological science into the material of his sacred eloquence, in translating a thesis into a sermon, in making Aquinas a Lacordaire or Suarez a Bourdaloue. It would seem paradoxical at first sight to affirm any difficulty whatsoever. Truth is one and the same whether couched in a syllogism or resonant in a period. Falsehood may assume a thousand disguises; but truth has but one expression upon its immobile features, one look in its sleepless eyes; eternally fixed upon eternal foundations, with unswerving gaze — the ideal of sphinxes, moored with shiftless fixedness upon the shifting sands of falsehood.

But the difficulty in question does not come from truth.   You have the same proportions of hydrogen and oxygen in the glacier as you have in the river, but in some cases it took geological ages, in all cases it involves the expenditure of immense energy, to strip ice of its accidental rigidity and frigidity and run it molten down the valleys of the world, conforming itself to every varying width and every varying depth of its proper channel. There is no substantial change in the truth, but its accidental form must put off the in- flexible austerity of science and assume the flexibility and warmth of eloquence.   In the famous statement of St. Augustine, which embodies the world-old tradition of oratory, theology puts a full stop after the first member; eloquence, leaving the commas, goes on to the end of the three clauses.   " Ut veritas pateat, ut veritas placeat, ut veritas moveat." That the truth may be clear; that the truth may be interesting; that the truth may be emotional.   (*De Doctrina Christ.* 4.)

The technical term is something that must be left in the lecture-room.   Science could scarcely exist without the technical term. Such terms constitute the shorthand of science.   One phrase in theology is sometimes

an index to volumes, condenses ages of
church history, expedites scientific discussion
and is the gravestone of a thousand heresies.
Pelagianism, transubstantiation, hypostasis,
circum-insession, and all the *terminative's*
and *formaliter's* of the theological disputa-
tion are absolutely essential to science, very
nearly fatal to eloquence. The reason is
not because shallow thinkers or careless students make the technical term a substitute
for knowledge and think they have theology
because they have mastered its language, as
though the mere murmuring of x, y, z, entitled one to a degree in algebra. A terminology is the scaffolding needed to erect the
temple of truth. A certain amount of acrobatic skill will enable one to scale its bare
boards or tread securely its precarious raft-
ers, but while irresponsible youths are playing hide-and-seek on the scaffolding, the
builders, resting on that necessary structure,
lay the stones of the temple in solidity.

It is not, therefore, because of its abuse
that terminology is unserviceable to eloquence; it is precisely because of its scientific
utility. Technical terms constitute a language, and a very difficult language. It is a
language which saves valuable time for the
teachers. It is comprehensive, precise, se-
verely intellectual, but it is a foreign lan-

guage to people who listen to sermons and
scarcely serviceable for even a congregation
of theologians.   Its very condensation
makes it indigestible within the brief time
given to the spoken word, and even the Bread
of the Lord must be leavened, though not
with the leaven of the Pharisees.   Sometimes the very terms of ascetical theology
likewise need leavening before being dis-
pensed to the multitude.   " Mortification "
and " the spiritual life " and " the interior
spirit " and " supernatural motives," these
and many another term that has come to us
from the good books we read, are stereotyped formulas of asceticism and may be idle
words for many hearers.

The sacred orator must melt down the
stereotyped and run his language into new
molds for his audience.   He must leave the
glacial period of science where " froze the
genial currents of his soul " and thaw out in
the pulpit.   Estimate, if you will, the energy
of heat required to convert a world of ice
into a sea of fire, and you will have some
idea of the labor required to change a small
quantity of theology into the palpitating flexibility of a sermon.   Modern inventions
have been able by high-pressure machines to
force air bubbles into baking dough and so
to shorten the leavening process by dispens-

ing with the slower release and permeation of yeasty vapors. The work calls for time and energy. If you shorten the time, you must increase the energy. Sometimes it is only after years of thought and familiarity with the solid truth of theology that it has become light and wholesome for public consumption in the pulpit; sometimes the intense application of special study will force at once technicality and density into freedom and grace; but always either by expenditure of more time or more energy in the mastery of thought, must the prime matter of truth be made to doff the form of science and assume the form of art.

Suppose you should try to bring home to the audience the personality of God. You would have visions from theology of pantheism and agnosticism. You would recall shattered fragments of discussion about hypostasis and the individual. Perhaps half-forgotten heresies would struggle into consciousness with other flotsam and jetsam. All that would be quite unleavened for the audience you have in mind, and you might say to yourself, " I will talk to my good people about going to Mass and confession." But perhaps with longer meditation you would feel that the personality of God might give a meaning to religious life, might com-

fort a lonely soul, might take prayer out of
the region of the clouds, making it, instead
of what would be deemed as senseless talking to the air, rather the loving converse with
one who knows and loves, whose ear is ever
at our lips, as Fr. Farrell puts it somewhere;
and moved by these many advantages your
thought of God's personality would shed its
technicalities.   Fr. Pardow was a preacher
who had in his life a vivid realization of the
personality of God and made many attempts
to formulate his knowledge for the pulpit.
He often tried to make his hearers realize
what he felt.   One illustration had some
success.   " A government," he would quote
or say, "is impersonal. 'I cannot shake
hands with the United States,' was the cry
of the soldier.   My Colonel is my government for me."   But Fr. Pardow's successful
attempt at making his audience realize God's
personality was closely allied to one which
Christ Himself used for a similar purpose.
Not far from where Fr. Pardow lived at
Poughkeepsie he saw on one of his walks an
incubator whose source of heat was an oil-
lamp.   His mind was ever alert to spiritual
analogies, and one suggested itself at once.
The lamp would represent the impersonal
idea of God as a force in the universe and
would be contrasted with the mother-hen, the

embodiment of the personal idea. The illustration is crude as here presented, but it was not so in his development of it, and his fine sense of humor was able in a delicate way to make much of the absurdity of an oil-lamp masquerading as a mother-hen. Whatever may be thought of it, it certainly was, with other explanations, effective in securing a realization of God's personality. One good, shrewd Irishman was full of the idea after the sermon, and prayer became for him a new thing. Another person wrote to Fr. Pardow in English which is rude but in enthusiasm which is unmistakable: " Dear Father on Good Friday night Will you please give us the Leture you gave down at the 16st Collige. About the Chicken who had a Mother. And the Chicken who had the Incubator for a Mother. Father I am trying to get some of the Boys who do not know what the inside of our church look like and I know if they was to hear about the Chicken it would set them to think of God in this holy season of Lent." The note is unsigned.

Assuredly it would seem to be a far cry from the personality of God to an incubator, yet it made the writer of that note think of God, and with the zeal of an apostle he wanted the boys to think the same way. Similar but greater enthusiasm was aroused,

we may feel sure, by the supreme eloquence
of, " Jerusalem, Jerusalem, thou that killest
the Prophets, and stonest them that are sent
to thee, how often would I have gathered together thy children, as the hen doth gather
her chickens under her wings, and thou
wouldest not? "   We feel the Great Theologian and Sacred Orator would not have dis-
dained the incubator with its homely oil-
lamp.   There are few technical terms in the
eloquence of the Gospels.

Scientific truth differs from artistic truth
in its presentation.   The truths of science
are general.   Science works from the particular and concrete back to the general and
abstract.   The truths of art are embodied in
the concrete.   Contrary to science, art begins with the ideal and works toward a concrete presentation.   Geometry will reduce a
flower-garden to a blueprint; landscape gar-
dening will turn lines into borders and blank
spaces into mosaics of flowers.   The archi-
tect must have his blueprint to keep him from
going wrong, but art finds its realization in
the cathedral.   Science gives an anatomical
chart; art produces a statue.   Principles, de-
ductions, conclusions, classification, systems,
these are processes of science, and valuable
they all are for art, but all these operations
are facing the abstract and general.   Art

faces the concrete and particular, and after
its survey of heaven and earth it is not content until it gives " airy nothings a local habi-
tation and a name."   Science is ever climbing up the tree of Porphyry; art is ever
climbing down it.

Apply all this now to theology and preaching.   Anyone can see the two opposite processes exemplified in such words as Corluy's
Spicilegium Dogmaticum, and in most com-
mentators who are looking to the essential
truths of Scripture.   The Sermon on the
Mount is reduced to a series of general prop-
ositions where everything local, particular,
and concrete is set aside to arrive at the essence, to classify the product and codify a
system.   Take again the sermon on prayer
(Luke 11).   " Lord, teach us to pray," said
one of His disciples.   The first part of the
sermon advises the recitation of Our Father;
then follows a famous parable, a picture with
all its details, local, actual, and contemporary; the perfection of the concrete.   In the
crucible of science these details are all swept
away.   " Friend, lend me three loaves," is
generalized into " prayer."   " If he shall
continue knocking," is the artistic expression
for the scientific " persevering."   So with
the rest: the midnight hour, the shut door,
the children in bed, the continual knocking,

the reluctant rising, the triumph of the visitor, all disappear, and this piece of eloquence becomes a theological conclusion asserting " the efficacy of persevering prayer; for if selfishness and indolence yield to importunity among creatures, how much more is this true of God? "

Here is what becomes of that particular drama in scientific garb: " The main circumstances therefore are: sudden, unthought of, sense of imperative need, obliging to make what seems an unseasonable and unreasonable request, which, on the face of it, offers difficulties and has no claim upon compliance. . . . It points to continued importunity which would at last obtain what it needs." (*Edersheim*: *Life of Christ, II, 240.*)

Think a moment of all the great truths of faith which have been embodied in exact terms and defined and made perspicuous by reason and authority; and set them side by side with the gospel which is sacred eloquence and from which these great truths arose; and you will understand the marked difference between the scientific and artistic form of the same truth. The providence of God and the lilies of the field, the papal supremacy and the keys, the infallibility and the rock and the sheep, unity and the one

fold, grace and the wedding garment, charity
and the Good Samaritan, humility and the
little child, perfect contrition and the prodigal, torments of hell and unquenchable fire
without a single drop on a parched tongue —
there is no need of prolonging the catalog.
The parable, the example, the story, the sim-
ilitude, the epigram, the brief description,
these are rarely employed in the text-books
of science, where clearness of truth is looked
for: " ut veritas pateat." These, however,
always enshrine the truths of eloquence
where the charm of truth is sought for:
" ut veritas placeat."

Finally, scientific truth is unemotional.
Earnestness may galvanize a chapter of
Suarez into momentary life, but that life is
only galvanic and extrinsic. It comes from
flashing eye and thrilling tone and vigorous
gesture, but the truth itself is unemotional.
Science wants it so. It excludes emotion as
distracting and out of place. Imagine a professor of geometry tearfully and exultantly
announcing in tremulous tones his Q. E. D.
Science does not amplify, does not enforce its
truths with emotional vehemence, does not
perorate. If you do not understand, it gives
another proof, or another exposition.
When you catch the fact or principle, the
work of science is done. The mind is

equated with objective realities; it is vested with the truth. You have a perfect mental fit. It is no part of science to comment on the beauty of the vesture or its goodness. It has already passed on to fit your mind with another truth. Ah, but art does not pass on. In its mental vestures, art dwells upon their beauty and is attracted or repelled by their goodness or evil. The truth of art is transfigured by the imagination into a thing of beauty and is shown to be stained with evil or glowing with goodness, because in eloquence the truth must pass from the mind through the imagination to the heart: " ut veritas pateat, ut veritas placeat, ut veritas moveat."

One glance of the opened eye sees the flash of truth; the gaze must be riveted to behold its beauty; the look must be fascinated to thrill with truth's emotion. So the orator amplifies and is diffuse. He deepens the dark shadows of the picture that you may hate it more and more; he emphasizes the light areas that you may like the picture more and more. He will never be content with your merely seeing it. Science flows on like a stream, steadily, constantly, presenting new stretches of water to our gaze. Eloquence swells and heaves, tosses itself in anger or subsides into .peace, like the sea, which spreads the same waters before us in a thousand varying forms. In a sense, therefore, the sacred orator must know theology better than the theologian. He will not be content with a surface knowledge but will feel the pulse of truth and listen to its heart-beat. He will get down below terms to realities. Before his imagination general truth will marshal the multitudes of their individuals, and disclose the significant individual which will best represent the class. His knowledge of theological truths will widen out into the myriad relations and analogies in history, art, and nature wherein the profoundest theology may be presented and illustrated in the simplest object-lesson familiar to every audience. Part of Chesterton's success consists in his power of bringing his philosophy, as much as he has, down to the lowest common denominator. He sees philosophy in the veriest trifles of life. I know, too, a chemist who has so mastered his science that I really believe he could give a complete course in chemistry with experiments and illustrations from the stains and paints and what not of his room. So must the preacher have mastered his theology for the pulpit. He must be able to see sermons in everything, discern the great round orb of God's truth reflected in countless shades and tints from all the creatures in God's universe.

His truth will be apostolic, will become all things to all men to save all, will avoid the scientific language which appeals to the expert and the trite language which appeals to no one, will keep his language from degenerating into mere symbols, and so will be ever on the lookout in realms of the imagination for new forms in which to body forth the old thoughts.   The truth of the orator must be apostolic; it must win its way by beauty and charm and ensure its progress to its destination, the human heart, by filling itself with emotion, by manifesting its goodness or evil. " Ut veritas pateat, ut veritas placeat, ut veritas moveat."

IV

THE IMAGINATION OF THE SPEAKER

IV

THE IMAGINATION OF THE SPEAKER

A PREACHER was once delivering a sermon. There was no doubt of his earnestness. He was painfully earnest. His cheeks were hot; his eyes filled with tears; his voice faltered, and he almost broke down with the excess of his own tremendous efforts. Yet all the while he left his audience unthrilled. " He was insulated," as one of his audience put it. He had an audience overcritical perhaps and more than ordinarily intellectual. A simpler congregation might have kindled at the sight of the flames even though they were beyond the radius of the heat. This incident, which may no doubt be typical of many, raises the interesting question whether earnestness and sincerity are sufficient to insure success in preaching. The speaker must be sincere and earnest; but is that enough? Must he not look to it that his warmth and energy leap

over into the hearts before him? Even if
he weep according to Horace's prescription,
will he make others weep unless they are
thrilled with the conviction that the occasion
demands their tears? The mere spectacle
of a weeping orator; the emphatic assertion
that they too should weep, however earnestly
proclaimed, these are not always adequate
means to elicit tears. The speaker must not
be insulated. If his words are not good
conductors of his own passionate energy, he
may succeed in concentrating attention upon
himself and not upon his subject. Like an
acrobatic fiddler who plays a sonata with one
string while balancing himself on a wire, he
himself is more interesting than his tune.
He might just as well be earnest in a foreign
language, if his own language fails to translate his emotion. Let a speaker deliver in
English with all conceivable sincerity and
earnestness the thesis of St. Thomas on the
intensity of Christ's sufferings in His Passion; let him even strip the discussion of
purely technical terms, and he will communi-
cate some of his fire to those who listen, but
not surely as much as does Newman in the
close of his sermon, *Mental Sufferings of
Our Lord in His Passion*. Newman's reasons are largely the same as those of St.
Thomas, but his handling, of course, is dif-

ferent. It is the difference between science and art. (Cf. Chap. III.)

No preacher whether in his rôle as teacher or as apostle will rest content with a style or manner of presentation which will not reach his audience effectively. Even with one's best endeavor's the resistance to one's force will in some minds and hearts be too great. So not until the orator has done his best to wing his thoughts with living energy for all, will he lay the flattering unction to his soul that certain sections at least will appreciate his efforts. No teacher worthy of the name will cater to parts only of his class. He tries to reach all even though he may feel that some are not brought into contact with his message. No apostle will rest content with less than the ideal: " Yes, verily, their sound has gone forth into all the earth, and their words unto the ends of the whole world." The preacher with the spirit of an apostle will not be satisfied with a way of preaching that reaches a few, when a little more zeal would carry his words to a wider circle. Tolerance should be the attitude of charitable critics who will suppose a man has done his best and is doing his best to make his apostolic teaching sweep the whole horizon of his audience. Tolerance would be no virtue but perhaps an encouragement to easy indifference if it should cause a preacher to congratulate himself on a thirty-fold harvest when some improvement in composition and delivery might realize for him a hundred-fold.   Premature tolerance has overloaded the pulpit with arrested mediocrities.

The problem of preaching would be very much simplified if it could be stated in the terms, " Be earnest."   One wonders why we have not countless fine preachers when the course of oratory can be put in so brief a compass.   What would such a precept signify if transferred to other arts?   Give a man a hammer and a chisel with a block of marble and tell him, " Be powerful."   Put him before a piano and say, " Be thrilling." Provide him with canvas and paints and earnestly exhort him to be masterful.   Your Milton, I fear, will be mute and inglorious and will be buried with his poems unwritten. He is afire with lyrics and epics, but cannot stammer a line because he knows not how to practise his art.   He is a dynamo without a live conducting wire.

Quintilian's formula for eloquence is often quoted: " Pectus est quod disertos facit." Not all who quote take care to look up what the rhetorician means.   He is discussing the topic of ex-tempore speaking and remarks that those who are aroused by some powerful feeling, do not lack for words. When the passion cools down, the thoughts disappear and the words with them. "Therefore," says Quintilian, "we must conceive those pictures of things, which are called phantasms, and keep before our eyes and draw down into our hearts, everything of which we are to speak, persons, topics, hopes, fears. For it is the heart and energy of soul which makes speakers eloquent." The context not only furnishes us with an understanding of Quintilian's meaning, but tells us what he considered the best means of acquiring eloquence. That means is the imagination of the speaker. It is there the speaker must go to find an apt medium to transfer the warmth of his own heart to the hearts of his hearers. His words will flame with the earnestness he himself feels. His thoughts will leap from him, winged with force enough to reach the ear that waits to receive the message. If anyone can fill the hearers with pictures rather than words, with feelings as well as ideas, it will be he who does not merely understand his subject, but sees it, gets a vision of it, as Quintilian says. Even such may not always succeed in embodying their visions in their language but they are more likely to do so than others. The interesting speaker must have a good imagination.

A speaker cannot exhibit the things of which he speaks and usually has no representations or pictures of his topic. He cannot display to his audience a prodigal in a pigsty or give a moving-picture of the conversion of St. Paul. The speaker, however, can and does awaken these pictures in the imagination of those who listen to him. He keeps their " inward eye " as busy with views as he keeps their ears quivering with vibrations of sound. The speaker who makes people see things when he talks, has an imagination in the sense of which it is spoken of here.

" It is a great mistake," writes Storrs in *Preaching without Notes,* quoting Choate, " to think anything too profound or rich for a popular audience. No train of thought is too deep, subtle or grand, but the manner of presenting it to their untutored minds should be peculiar. It should be presented in an anecdote or sparkling truism or telling illustration or stinging epithet; always in some concrete form, never in a logical, abstract or syllogistic shape." This concrete presentation is another way of stating what is called here the speaker's imagination. The necessity of such a faculty no one will deny unless it be one who is frightened by the word imagination and conjures up at its appearance such unsubstantial things as dreams. But

the speaker's imagination is not the passive
faculty which fills the day with reveries and
crowds the nights with a vast assortment of
weird visions. If imagination meant dream-
ing, there would be no occasion for discussing its development. A quiet corner and a
good meal and a leisure half-hour would fill
the head with an endless succession of pictures, and for a more startling display by
night recourse might be had to sundry well-
known promoters of indigestion.

The imagination in the speaker which will
arouse the audience, is an active and aggres-
sive faculty. It is under the control of the
speaker and can be wielded at will. It differs from the imagination in its passive state,
as a speaking or writing vocabulary differs
from a reading vocabulary. Innumerable
are the words we understand, and readily understand, when we turn over the pages of a
book, but few of that host respond to our call
when we set ourselves to compose. It is
easy to follow a novelist through all the
scenes he presents; it is easy to follow the
aimless wanderings of day-dreaming or
night-dreaming, but it is something different
to evoke such scenes at will in response to
the needs of the speaker or writer. Then
the " inward eye " seems stricken blind. It
can dwell without difficulty on the moving-

pictures supplied by others; it finds it very hard to summon up visions in its own mind. To be concrete, to leave the general and indefinite for the particular and definite, to illumine a subject by an apt illustration, to make a thought strike home with the help of a significant detail, make it attractive in a novel guise or make it vivid in a dramatic presentation, all these actions do not come easy; they demand a vigorous power on the part of the writer.

It is usual to recommend the reading of fiction as a means to develop the imagination. Undoubtedly fiction does help and will give some exercise to this useful faculty, yet fiction is not entirely satisfactory. It leaves the reader too passive and has not produced results at all proportionate to its use. The wide reading of fiction should have supplied us with an abundance of imaginative speakers, but we rather suffer from a dearth of them. Others have recommended poetry as a developer of the imagination, and much may be said in its favor. The poet is not diffuse; he is brief and suggestive, and the reader who would appreciate must be active and force his own imagination to see what the poet dimly yet pregnantly outlines. Again the poet feels compelled by his office to present his thoughts in an imaginative garb. Poetry is a new language, heightened and colored by its contents, more intense and more emotional than ordinary prose. The one who adopts the language of poetry feels compelled to make use of metaphor, simile, condensed description, and other means which bring visions to the readers.

If anyone has a prejudice against reading profane poetry or does not find its subjects attractive, he might have recourse to the poetry of the Bible, where together with sublime and holy thoughts available for the pulpit, he will find the use of the imagination in its most excellent form. From one point of view indeed Hebrew poetry offers the best opportunity for developing the imaginative faculty. The speaker should have an imagination subdued to his control, responsive to his mastery. The concrete world should lie conquered at his feet and the created universe should be ready to rise promptly at his bidding. Now the Hebrew imagination, in its wide range and in its freedom and mastery of the world of sense, is certainly supreme among ancient literatures and has most largely opened the way for the bold and sublime flights of the modern imagination. Modern readers often fail to find sublimity in Homer where ancient critics rejoiced in it. They find pleasure in his fidelity to nature

and his picture of man's life, but their acquaintance with the language and facts of
revelation seems to render them less appreciative of Homer's sublimity which for the ancients was usually found in the movements
and acts of the gods.   The imagination of
Homer and the Greeks, and the same is true
of the Latins, was conditioned and restricted
by their trivial and grotesque cosmogony.
The waters could not rise higher than their
source.   Homer's imagination was hope-
lessly cramped by the narrow horizon which
mythological traditions offered him.   The
battle of the gods and the shaking of Jove's
ambrosial locks, the leaping of Neptune's
chariot over the sea, the descent into Hades
in the Odyssey, and other well-known passages, fall short of sublimity in our minds.
In every case there are elements or circumstances of the description which keep it near
the   earth.   The   poet's   imagination   is
clogged in its flight by the weight of the
earth.   His gods may be bigger than men;
they are not other than men.   Their actions,
their abodes have a mathematical extension
and increase; they do not rise above the limitations of matter.   In most cases the deities
of Homer are dwarfed in our view by his
presentation.   Neptune is not larger than
the ocean over which he rides.   The Sun-

God loses his sublimity by being wroth over the loss of a herd of cattle and threatening to refuse to shine unless vengeance is taken on the famishing followers of Ulysses. The other gods dwarf themselves to birds and animals.

How different with the Hebrew! The first chapter of *Genesis* effected the emancipation of the Hebrew imagination. Longinus recognized the sublimity of the Bible story of creation. The stupendous words of God, " Let there be light," were not simply a revelation of the fact of creation; they revealed the power and magnificence of the Creator. He was not a larger man; He was a Being of a different order who flooded the universe with light by one word. That scene never left the imagination of the Hebrews. They began their writings on a plane infinitely above Greek or Latin or other pagans. Their horizon went beyond the farthest stars. They did not look up to but looked down upon creation because they saw it through the gaze of the Creator. " The whole world before thee is as a least grain in the balance and as a drop of the morning dew," says Wisdom; and the Psalmist cries, " In the beginning, O Lord, Thou foundest the earth; and the heavens are the work of Thy hands. They shall perish, but Thou remainest; and all of them shall grow old like a garment; and as a vesture Thou shalt change them." "And all the hosts of the heavens," writes Isaias, "shall pine away and the heavens shall be folded together as a book; and all their host shall fall down as a leaf falleth from the vine and fig-tree." This coign of vantage over creation was never occupied by the pagan imagination. Pagans had no outlook which could dwarf the world to a dewdrop and cast aside the universe as a worn-out garment or roll it up like a manuscript.

What a sense of mastery such a position gave the Hebrews! It put them, it is true, far below God, but far above nature. They played with time and space. "If I take my wings," sings the Psalmist, "early in the morning and dwell in the uttermost parts of the sea, even there also shall Thy hand lead me and Thy right-hand hold me." In the Book of Job, the power of God is set forth in a sublime fashion and with easeful mastery. The weakness of man is contrasted with the might of the Creator. "Where wast thou when I laid the foundations of the earth? Who laid the corner-stone thereof when the morning stars praised me together and all the sons of God made joyful melody? Who shut up the sea with doors . . . when

I made a cloud the garment thereof and wrapt it in a mist in swaddling bands? I set my bounds around it and made it bars and doors; and I said: Hitherto thou shalt come and shalt go no further and here thou shalt break thy swelling waves." Nothing perhaps so well illustrates the complete sway of the Hebrew imagination over the world as such a passage where the earth has a cornerstone and the sea swaddling bands and bars and doors. How insignificant man becomes! " Against a leaf that is carried away with the wind," cries Job to God, " Thou showest Thy power; Thou pursuest a dry straw." " Behold even the moon doth not shine, and the stars are not pure in His sight. How much less man that is rottenness and the son of man who is a worm." How mighty is God! " He stood and measured the earth," declares Habacuc. " He beheld and melted the nations, and the ancient mountains were crushed to pieces. The hills of the world were bowed down by the journeys of His eternity." His wisdom is marvelously delineated in Proverbs: " When He prepared the heavens I was present; when with a certain law and compass He enclosed the depths; when He established the skies above and poised the fountains of water; when He compassed the sea with its bounds and set a

law to the waters that they should not pass
their limits; when He balanced the foundations of the earth, I was with Him forming
all things and was delighted every day, playing before Him all times."   His anger is
magnificent in Wisdom: " And His zeal
will take armor and He will arm the creature
for the revenge of His enemies.   He will
put on justice as a breastplate and will take
true judgment instead of a helmet.   He will
take equity for an invincible shield and He
will sharpen His severe wrath for a spear,
and the whole world shall fight with Him
against the unwise.   Then shafts of lightning shall go directly from the clouds, as
from a bow well bent; they shall be shot out
and shall fly to the mark."

A great deal of time has been given to this
point, more than most readers perhaps will
think necessary, but the numerous quotations
can be amply justified, first because they show
how the Hebrew imagination has subdued all
matter to its mastery, when elevated by Genesis to the outlook of the Creator; then next
these many passages will help the speaker to
win the same heights and attain the same
control in his own imaginative work.   Take
the last passage quoted with its magnificent
images, made possible by the viewpoint of
Hebrew poetry.   Will not a speaker who

has lifted himself aloft by means of such imaginings be able to hover above his own thought-world and make it serve him? Archimedes wanted a place to stand on in order with his lever to move the earth. The speaker schooled in poetry, especially Hebrew poetry, has such a place for his fulcrum. He is above matter; he contemplates it in the vast sweep of his commanding gaze; he sways it with his slightest touch and raises it to heights undreamt of by minds confined to earth.

What a help all that will be to the orator when he is rearing the structure of his thought! A few years ago I heard two preachers and each of them stood outside of and above his ideas and built them up into a massive oratorical structure on great lines. Monsignor Benson, in speaking of the sixth word of our Lord from the Cross, described Calvary as the keystone of an arch one curve of which went back to creation and the other reached out through the centuries since Christ and sank into the darkness of the future. " Consummatum est " was the keystone which Christ put upon the completed work of our Redemption. The whole passage was magnificent and possessed an imaginative unity and grandeur of feeling which is not found in the printed version of the discourse.

The speaker seemed to have built that arch in the glow of his imagination out of the materials which he had mastered and could manipulate as he desired. The other preacher who marshaled his thoughts in great masses as a general guides his army was Father Vaughan. The passage I refer to was in a lecture given in Carnegie Hall, New York City. The lecturer brought together as in a huge drama the conflicting philosophies of the day and their solutions of present evils. The scene opened in dramatic fashion with the iterated question to the watchman in Isaias: "Watchman, what of the night?" Pessimism, as one watchman, gave its answer. Then optimism gave its answer from the watch-tower. Their promises were rehearsed; their failure shown. "The morning cometh, also the night." This part of the discussion was brought to a striking close by an epigram. "Optimism forgets the fall of man; pessimism forgets the redemption of man." Then the speaker introduced another watchman of the tower of the Vatican. Pope Pius X, with his philosophy, "instaurare omnia in Christo." After explaining the application of the Christian solution to the world's evils, the lecturer concluded his drama by an eloquent apostrophe to the Crucifix. The whole passage was bound together in close dramatic unity, although inattentive or less thoughtful listeners might forget the plot in the development of the details. At no time, however, did the speaker's grasp fail and he showed complete control of all the entrances and exits of the thought divisions, governing all like a stage director. If the study of Hebrew poetry with its royal sway and mastery of the universe can help every speaker to be such as Fr. Vaughan and Mgr. Benson, and to stand above their thoughts and group them and marshal them effectively, then such a study should form a part of every speaker's curriculum.

A speaker who can rise above his subject and contemplate it in all its ramifications is the one who can strike out from his imagination those novel presentations of thought which are to be found in great writers. By some they are technically called *fictiones*. They embrace such allegories as Addison usually resorted to or such methods for novelty and force which are found in Newman's "Second Spring," where he imagines his hearers viewing from another planet the disturbances at the establishment of the English Hierarchy, or where he represents Bishop Milner prophesying the first synod. The famous speech of the Russian in the " Present Position of the Catholics " may be referred to the same category. The eloquent oath of Demosthenes is another example of an imaginative *fictio*. No speaker can hope to strike out these ingenious and effective methods without an imagination, and a complete mastery of the matter is an essential prerequisite. Hebrew poetry, especially the Psalms, have splendid instances of such pictures. Take the twenty-eighth Psalm. The whole world is transformed by the Psalmist into a huge temple where men are to bring sacrifice and offer adoration, a temple thrilling with the power and presence of God, for across the temple's floor, which is here the land of Palestine, comes a thunderstorm. That for the Psalmist is the " voice of the Lord," which sounds, first on the waters of the sea, then over the cedars of Libanus, then over the desert and woods, and accompanied by the " flame of fire," reverberates and reëchoes in the cloud-built arches and blue vault of the world-wide Holy of Holies.

V

INTEREST FROM EMOTIONS

V

INTEREST FROM EMOTIONS

A SERMON without emotions in it will be as interesting as a lecture in theology. The vast majority of men are impatient of reasoning. They are enthusiastic if the speaker flames with indignation or kindles with triumphant joy. They are even contented with the pathos which elicits their tears. To reason or to follow reasoning is hard; to feel is spontaneous and easy. That is why an audience dwindles away or suffers in silent patience during the dry discussion of a metaphysician, but crowds the tent and shouts vociferously with some emotional revivalist. How is it that modern teachers and text-books of oratory ignore this fact or give but scant attention to it? The chapter on emotions used to be one of the most important in rhetoric. The books of to-day have omitted the chapter. In some schools it still remains, but rather as a fossil relic of old times than as a vital factor in the teaching of oratory.

73

Several answers may be given to the question why the topic of emotions has been neglected. First of all, outside of the traditional philosophy of the schools, modern writers are in complete confusion on the subject of emotions or feelings. There is no agreement about their nature or their classification. Some advance in knowledge has been made on the physical side of the emotions. The muscles, the nerves, and the brain have been investigated as they vibrated with emotion, but we are not much nearer in that way to the nature of the emotion than we should be to the nature of electricity by ascertaining the chemical constituents of the wire which carried the current. Some have equipped man with a new faculty of soul for the registering of the emotions, but our philosophers (Maher, *Psychology*, pp. 221–228) are able to show that the senses, intellect, and will can do all the work of the emotions without the necessity of a new faculty.

Modern rhetoricians are unable to say how to appeal to the emotions if they do not know what they are or where they originate. Scholastic philosophy with its source in Aristotle has clear notions on the nature and causes of emotion. The pleasure arising from the contemplation of what is beautiful is by many styled esthetic emotion. Modern Scholastic philosophy has followed St. Thomas in making the feeling excited by the beautiful a pleasure or intense satisfaction of the cognitive faculties, either of the senses, imagination, and intellect, or of the intellect alone. Philosophers differ on the question of what are the objective elements of beauty, although most agree in the elements of luster, order, unity in variety; but the philosophers who represent the tradition of the schools, all assert that the subjective effect of beauty is a special pleasure found in the act of knowing and does not belong to the appetitive faculty. " Beauty," teaches St. Thomas, " regards knowledge." (S. I, 5, 4.) " It belongs to beauty," he tells us, " to satisfy by its sight and contemplation." (S. I, 2ᵃᵉ, 27, 1.) According to him the objective elements of beauty are " perfection, right proportion, and luster."

When speakers are told to arouse emotions, it is not meant that their object is to display the beauty of their thoughts. Beauty is not excluded from oratory, as will be seen, but it holds a subordinate, though helpful, place. The emotions of which oratory speaks, are excited by good and evil, not by beauty. The emotions of oratory are aroused in the will, not in the intellect. The good or evil must be presented through the senses and imagination if the emotions are to be thrilling and effective. Real, vigorous emotions find a responsive vibration in the whole man. Purely abstract and intellectual considerations of good or evil do not give that energetic impulse which the orator desires for his purpose. There is a physical element in emotions and should be if they are to exercise their full effect, and that is the reason why the speaker must reach his hearers' imaginations. If they could see the evils of intemperance, they might be resolved to be temperate. The speaker cannot display on the stage a horrible example to disgust his hearers. He endeavors to present his ideas to the imagination in such a way that in every one who listens, he may excite the horror of the actual spectacle. That emotion, then, has a physical basis and will be most effective in eloquence. If the orator can make the flesh creep, he will make the soul shrink. Goose-flesh will bring a heart-chill.

Besides being unable or unwilling to locate the faculty of the emotions, modern writers do not seem fully to understand the nature of emotions in themselves. They do not clearly distinguish between esthetic emotions and appetitive emotions, between the restful satisfaction of the mind in knowing a beautiful object and the tendency of the appetite and will toward an object which is good. These rhetoricians would appear to reduce all emotions to vague sentimentality. They do not grasp what robust love or hatred really means and even their idea of the esthetic emotion of beauty is perhaps not much different from the satisfaction of a warm fire or the savor of well-cooked food. Scholastic philosophy has clear-cut views on these points, and no one who teaches or studies oratory can safely neglect them. Beauty, philosophy tells us, is associated with good. The very thing which awakens the emotions of good and evil, may be and often is vested by the speaker in beauty of language and thought. Yet the beauty is one thing and the good another. The emotions of the will are self-seeking. Even the highest kind of altruistic love must begin in self-seeking, although it finally succeed in purifying itself of all baser elements. On the other hand, the esthetic emotion awakened by beauty is unselfish. Thousands will share in the beauty of a landscape. You will not object to the whole world admiring the beauty of your fruit, but in the case of a single apple you may say with the small boy, enamored of its good, " There ain't going to be no core."

Animals have emotions of love or hate, fear
or courage, but do not manifest any sensibil-
ity to beauty. If you see your dog on the
seashore gazing, as you think, pensively over
the " endless book of the landless blue," believe it no satisfaction of beauty. It is most
likely a piece of meat in the offing of the
dog's imagination. The esthetic emotions
arising from beauty differ essentially from
the emotions of appetite and will awakened
by good.

The truth is, as Aquinas has said, that
" good has the nature of an end or final
cause; beauty that of a formal cause."
Good is kinetic; beauty is static, and in this
brief statement of the ultimate truth in this
matter is found the chief reason and necessity for arousing the emotions. Beautiful
thoughts, dazzling theories, entrancing style,
charm of voice and language, please indeed
and thrill, but there in their apprehension
the energy spends itself because that is the
complete and full effect of beauty. Beauty
arrests; it fascinates; it awes perhaps; it sur-
prises; it entrances, and there it stops, having done its full duty. Contemplation is the
homage that the majesty of beauty claims.
Not so with good. Good is kinetic. It
makes the appetite restless; it provokes a
struggle; it draws the faculty to itself; it will

permit no rest until it is possessed.   Confusion in this matter often comes from the fact that the same object has beauty and goodness, but for different reasons, and also from the fact that beauty, being a perfection of the faculty of knowing, is a good for that faculty and so becomes the object of the will's desire. It would, however, lead us too far from our present purpose to go into the metaphysics of beauty.   It is enough to have shown that good is kinetic and beauty static in its effects, and from that fundamental distinction we have the diverse rôles which these elements play in oratory.

Why is it necessary that the orator should arouse the emotions and make the will act? Is it not enough for him to show the truth? Sad experience has repeatedly taught that knowledge is not enough.   The speaker who thinks it sufficient to show the truth of a statement and then expects to have results, is a victim of the same fallacy which dreams that to know is to will, that education of the mind means morality.   Even supposing the speaker can clearly demonstrate the truth so that there will be no doubt remaining in his hearers, that will not be enough for him. The speaker, if he is not a mere scientific lecturer and theorist, has always in view something to be done, some practical out-

come of his words. Everyone knows the
vast chasm which yawns between theory and
practice, and there is only one bridge across
that chasm, that is the goodness of the practice or, what is the same thing, the evils of
its omission. Show the good and if the will
of man does not follow it, the orator will not
be at fault. He has proposed to the will the
only thing which can make the will move.
If there is no response, then his message has
not gone home or the freedom of man's will
has checked the action.

The practical corollaries, therefore, which
usually do and almost always must follow
from eloquence, necessitate the arousing of
emotions, even when the mind is perfectly
convinced by evident truth. Yet unhappily
how often in public speaking it is impossible
from the nature of the question or from the
time at the speaker's disposal to make the
truth more than probable to the listener. In
that case when there is doubt, it is the will
which must decide. Full evidence alone ne-
cessitates the decision of the mind. Where
such evidence is not forthcoming, the will
makes the intellect accept the truth. There
again motives must be offered, the good or
evil of the proposed truth must be presented;
in a word, the emotions must be aroused.

The need, therefore, of emotions in oratory is due to the practical results and probable conclusions with which the speaker has to deal.   There are two needs in appearance, but one in reality.   In both cases it is the necessity for action which demands the awakening of the emotions.   The quest of good is the energy of the will, the impelling force of man's acts, whether it be the act of the will which determines the intellect to assent to a probable truth or the act which determines any other faculty to respond to the orator's appeal for practical application of the truths he has established.   " Bonum habet rationem causae finalis."   (Good has the nature of a final cause.)   " Pulchrum proprie pertinet ad rationem causae formalis."   (Beauty properly has the nature of a formal cause.) " Bonum dicitur id quod simpliciter complacet appetitum."   (Good we call that which directly satisfies the appetite.)   " Pulchrum dicitur id cujus ipsa apprehensio placet."   (Beauty we call that which by its very knowledge gives pleasure.)   These are some phrases from Aquinas which sum up in his pregnant and clear way the essential distinctions between good and beauty and furnish the student of oratory with a rule for the use of these two elements in eloquence.

The speaker will not, however, disdain beauty.   Truth for him is an absolute neces-

sity because he must reach man's mind; good
for him is an absolute necessity because he
demands action and therefore will; beauty,
if not an absolute requisite of the process of
persuasion, is at least a great help.   For the
artist, beauty is essential because he must
give intellectual pleasure.   If, above and beyond that pleasure, his painting or poem conveys a lesson or impels to action, such a result is not called for by the requirements of
his art.   A picture of a flower or a poem on
a flower may do no more than re-create, in
paint or words, the actual flower which eye
and mind find pleasurable in nature, and the
painting and verse are works of art and em-
bodiments of beauty, even if the artist goes
no further than that.

The orator, however, must go farther; and
with him, while the beautiful is distinctly
subordinate to truth and good, it is useful
and   perhaps   even   absolutely   necessary,
though not to the extent that it is in other
arts.   We say other arts, because oratory is
a fine art and as such would demand some
beauty.   It is not, however, to be forgotten
that the beautiful is not anything vague and
unsubstantial, sickly and sentimental.   It is,
in the words of Kleutgen, " the natural perfection of a thing made resplendent in its
manifestation."   Others call the beautiful

"the luster or splendor of truth." It is
truth with a shining morning face. The orator finds his truth ignored or unappreciated,
overlaid with the dust of neglect or not recognized because it receives but casual attention in this busy world. The orator must
so speak the truth that he who runs may hear
and see. His audience will not be with him
long, and he must remove the tarnish of truth
and reveal its shining beauty. Perhaps
prejudice or antipathies may cloud his hearers' minds, and before the goodness of his
truth can win its way to affected wills, he
must make the full, round orb of truth dawn
upon the mind. Novelty, originality, fresh,
unhackneyed presentation of ideas, every le-
gitimate charm of language, whether named
or catalogued by rhetoricians or apparently
defying analysis, any new angle of truth, any
interesting view, in a word anything which
will awaken an indolent mind or arrest a
wandering mind or fascinate an inattentive
mind, any and all of these are to be highly
prized by the speaker, and they are all phases
of the beauty which will further him in his
aim to make truth reach home to the heart.
Truth is the engine; emotion arising from
good or evil is the energy which drives it on,
and interest or charm or beauty is the glis-
tening oil which makes every part work

smoothly. For his progress the orator requires all three. *Docere, delectare,* and *movere* have been handed down the ages as the three means for an orator to persuade. Truth, beauty, and goodness are the three graces of eloquence. Their combined powers make the message of the orator effective with the soul of man.

VI

MEMORY AS A TEST OF
INTEREST

VI

MEMORY AS A TEST OF INTEREST

IT is told of a priest of the Boston diocese, who is now no more, that he was complimented by one of his parishioners on a sermon. The priest was curious to know what truth it was that made so deep an impression, but all his questioning elicited no reply. Finally the parishioner admitted that he remembered nothing of what was said. " But you see, Father," he urged in defence, " it's just like this. My wife puts my shirt in water, soap and bluing, and though none of those articles remain when the washing is finished, the shirt is far better off for it all. And so am I for your sermon, though I don't recall anything of it."

In many cases it must be sadly confessed that the Sunday morning sermon is like the Monday morning washing. The effects remain for some time in both cases, but the causes have evaporated. Yet the preacher

is a teacher as well as a stimulant and is eager
to have his lessons abide though they should
also impart life and vigor in their delivery.
Can one find out what it is in a sermon which
will outlive the day of its preaching? Not
fully, of course, because there are many
freakish survivals in memory as well as outside of it which seem to have no particular
fitness entitling them to old age.

Still a voyage of discovery into the regions
of the memory will disclose here and there
some bit of land, whether a tiny island of
precarious volcanic origin or a more solid
and greater continent not yet submerged by
the waters of forgetfulness. For several
years, with a view to discovering the constituents of the surviving lands, a teacher of rhetoric has had his pupils write out three of
their earliest recollections of sermon truths.
The experiment showed much variety and
yet some marked uniformity in the traits of
remembered truths. Those interested may
perform the experiment for themselves and
see whether it corresponds with the results
obtained by the study of a reporter's memory.
Mr. James Douglas made the rounds of the
London churches and published his impressions of their preachers in the London *Morning Leader*. He afterwards gathered his
remarks into a book called *The Man in the*

Pulpit. Here we may study the survival of the memory's fittest.

The material for the experiment is not wholly suitable. Mr. Douglas went as a critic. Now a critic is not a normal listener. He stands on the side-lines, we may say. He has not thrown himself into the excitement of the game. He enters the church as the school-inspector does the class-room, not to learn with the docility and eager curiosity of a child but to examine and test and approve with the cold aloofness of a judge. Mr. Douglas is a journalistic critic, and that renders him less suitable still as a listener. The journalist looks for the striking and arresting points, the spice for his readers. Mr. Douglas finally is a stylist of a pronounced type.

Macaulay offered up sacrifices to truth on the altar of balance. Mr. Douglas looks as though he would be equally unmerciful for the sake of a metaphor. It is certainly interesting and extremely diverting to watch him working and weaving a city, a church, a voice, a face, a person into the devious pattern of a metaphor. The result is fascinating; it is Swinburne in prose (Mr. Douglas intensely admires Swinburne); it holds the reader entranced as the man does who keeps some half a dozen sharp, gleaming knives whirling through the air, but when the breathless performance is over, the reader is tempted to say, " juggling." Mr. Douglas likes to reduce a man or a scene to a common denominator. Such writing is indeed stimulating and diverting, but it is fanciful and often strained. We admire the ingenious dexterity of Mr. Douglas; we are not convinced.

To give an example of the London reporter as a stylist, like Swinburne in his alliteration, like the Pickwickian Jingle in his sentences, we may quote his description of Father Vaughan. The criticism is better than the style. " The sermon is simple, sensuous, passionate. Glowing eloquence poured hot from the heart. No notes, no manuscript. Well-built withal. A noble edifice of emotion harmoniously balanced and richly decorated with spontaneous phrase. No taint or trace of a metaphysical microbe, no pulpit pedantry. Lyrically free from the disease of thought. Throughout it throbs with the poignant pathos of Christ and Christians crucified. It is a bacchanal of rapturous agony and ecstatic anguish, a pæan of passion, joyous saturnalia of sorrow."

But to come to the question of what was remembered by Mr. Douglas. Despite his drawbacks as a listener, it might be said because of them, the experiment is worth making. Underneath the critic, the journalist and the stylist is human nature, and the man in the pulpit found in this man in the pew, a heavily armored, yet not impregnable listener. Even a reporter may on occasion be human and forget his profession.

Professors of the art of teaching tell us, and experience confirms their statements, that the teacher will make his pupils remember by repetition and by novelty, or interesting presentation. Mr. Douglas confirms this truth. Rev. Silas Hocking had " reiterative amplification of a simple phrase." " With the hammer of a phrase, he drives the nail of instruction into the board," says Mr. Douglas. Much of Father Vaughan's sermon too was hammered in by a refrain.

The first type of interesting presentation is the story. The example of this London reporter is hardly needed to prove that the story is a memory survival. Akin to the story are the facts and examples of history. Rev. R. J. Campbell, Father Vaughan, Monsignor Croke Robinson and others get parts of their sermons in the *Morning Leader* by their historical facts. Comparisons save others from forgetfulness and in that point the reporter's memory is like the more fallible memories of ordinary mortals. The simile is indispensable in the art of remembering sermons. "We have powder in our breasts," said Pastor Thomas Spurgeon, and we should probably never have known that way of describing our inflammable passions, had not the fluttering wings of the truth been fixed in a distracted memory by the shining point of an epigram, here crowned with the jewel of a comparison. Rev. Archibald Brown combines epigram, example and comparison and has succeeded in being very much remembered. On the peg of his text "he hangs a whole wardrobe of racy aphorisms, quaint quips and homely parables." Canon Newbolt is an "epigrammist" and proves his fitness to survive by many "flashing phrases" like, "castles in the air for the imagination to dwell in are better than pigstyes on the earth for sensuality to wallow in." Rev. J. H. Jowett unites many of the qualities already mentioned. His "delightful characteristic is his rich fertility of allusion and illustration, symbol and simile. He tells an anecdote with pungent humor, but his anecdotes are always apt and apposite."

So far, it might be said, it is external qualities which made the truth survive in the journalist memory. More important as preservers of truth are the internal qualities. Personality and sincerity, directness, absence of mere phrase making, avoidance of rhetorical flowers, these are qualities which this reporter harps on again and again, are qualities too which sent the truth living and quivering into his memory with vital vigor enough to survive the crush at the door after the services. Here is one statement out of a hundred very like it: "Just as his eyes save his face from insignificance, so his enthusiasm saves his oratory from conventionality. Personality can remove mountains and there is a flame in Hensley Henson's voice which sets his words on fire. He believes in his religion, his Church, and in himself. That is the one thing that completes the circuit between the pulpit and the pew. Without it sermons are corpses."

Yet personality has its dangers for one who would remember, and Mr. Douglas has repeatedly fallen victim to them. He remembers the man better than what he said. Is not that true of most of us? Emotion however is better than personality as a fixer of thoughts. Dr. Lorimer, the "famous New York preacher," is conspicuous for true feeling. "He does not read his sermons, and here I may say," writes Mr. Douglas, "that read sermons ought to be abolished. No, he preaches with fresh, not stale, emotions, and his words fall molten from his lips." Mr. Douglas is generous to the several American preachers he heard in London.

The last point to be mentioned as a crystallizer of lasting remembrances is actuality. This quality is responsible for the largest number of longest survivals of the many sermons this reporter heard. His ideal preacher has his " eye on the hour." The science of the day with its difficulties against revelation, the social questions pressing for solution, the thorny points of theology now torturing Protestants, the position of the Bible, the nature of Christ, the personality of God, all these questions make the reporter forget the *Morning Leader* and merge himself into the larger humanity for whom the soul is more than a newspaper. Other means made phrases or passages survive in the memory; actuality has preserved pages from oblivion.

What then will get your sermon beyond the church door into the paper and perhaps into a book? If Mr. Douglas may be taken as the type of a normal man, here is what you will have to do. Know the prejudices of the audience, if possible. They will remember what they like. Enlist the prejudices in your favor. Embody your truth in a story; illustrate it with a comparison; condense it into an epigram; reiterate it with persist-

ency.   Gather historical facts with which to
prove it.   Show that what you defend is a
living actual issue in the scientific, moral or
religious world of to-day.   Then if you have
a clear order, and enforce what you say with
sincerity, displayed in the flash of the eye, the
swing of the arm and the ring of the voice,
your truth will abide.   It will set the hearts
of your audience beating faster and so stimulate them as they hear, but more than that,
it will enrich their thoughts with new life-
blood and will continue to do good after the
echoes of your voice have died away.

VII

EWMAN AND THE ACADEMIC STYLE

VII

NEWMAN AND THE ACADEMIC STYLE

IN the last thirty years of Newman's life we have record of but four published sermons: one in 1866, which has been included in *Sermons on Various Occasions;* a memorial sermon in 1873 for J. R. Hope-Scott; and two sermons given at Oxford in 1880 and printed privately that same year. Newman became a Catholic in 1845 and by far the greater part of his Catholic sermons, to be found in the volume already mentioned and in *Discourses to Mixed Congregations,* were written during the first ten years of his Catholic life. In fact this latter volume was published in 1849, two years after his return from Rome where he had been with the exception of some months from the time of his conversion. The change of style which many have claimed to notice between his Catholic and Protestant sermons must have taken place very quickly. If we leave out of account the certainty and definiteness of doc-

trine and the newness of the doctrine, both
of which points most probably colored the
opinions of those who are not Catholic and
who do not keep the form and the subject-
matter sufficiently distinct, we may very well
doubt that there is the marked difference of
style so frequently proclaimed. The truth
seems to be that Newman's speaking style
gradually evolved into what we find in his
Catholic sermons.

The congregations and the occasions will
influence the handling of a topic in a sermon,
and Newman was too accomplished a writer
not to be deeply susceptible to the slightest
change in his listeners or their surroundings.
" Definiteness," he says in University Preaching, a lecture in the *Ideas of a University*,
" is the life of preaching.   A definite hearer,
not the whole world; a definite topic, not the
whole evangelical tradition; and, in like manner, a definite speaker."   He had already in
the same lecture insisted upon a definite purpose.   These principles of definiteness are
the basis of all speaking in the popular style,
which means speaking in an intelligible way,
not to a special class, not to the highly edu-
cated, not to the uneducated but to the people
of average education.   Newman's sermon
of *The Second Spring*, which serves as the
basis of this chapter, is academic and not

popular. No doubt, addressed as it was to a select audience, it should be academic. Very true; but as it likewise is a sermon disclosing many of Newman's characteristics, it may fairly be taken as typical of all his sermons, at least on the points examined.

A characteristic sermon of Newman's should not run counter to his own published principles on preaching and should fall in with his practice in the same art. From that point of view it may be stated with sufficient confidence that *The Second Spring* is characteristic of Newman's style and may be fitly chosen to exemplify his traits in the art of preaching.

The burden of Newman's teaching on the matter of preaching may be summed up in the word <u>definiteness</u>. That is the chief lesson he conveys when he treats professedly of preaching. *The Second Spring* is the most definite of sermons. If the time, place and persons concerned with this sermon were not known, the sermon itself would reveal them. " It is the first Synod of a new Hierarchy," near to " St. Michael's Day, 1850," when " a storm arose in the moral world," and the restored English Church was welcomed as " the lion greets his prey." The audience was made of " priests and religious and theologians of the school and canons " and " well

nigh twelve mitred heads " and " a Prince of
the Church."　The speaker is a convert, an
Oratorian who bears witness from without
of the contempt into which Catholicism had
fallen.　He feels the delicacy of his position
and touches every chord to which he knows
his hearers will respond and his touch is firm
and fearless.　Bishop Milner, the " vener-
able man, the Champion of God's ark in an
evil time," the glories of the English Church,
the Sees and the Saints of Old England, the
blood of English martyrs, the tender call to
" Mary, Mother of God, dear Lady, to go
forth into that North country which once was
her own," " the invocation of the same sweet
and powerful name " in the new St. Mary's,
these are the notes the new convert strikes,
and no life-long Catholic of the oldest family, of the most sacred traditions could have
chosen his topics better or given them more
affecting expression.

The Second Spring is then characteristic
in its definiteness and it has too a characteristic drawback that often accompanies Newman's definiteness.　On reading and reflection, we are conscious of the unity and the
singleness of aim in this as well as others of
Newman's sermons.　But on its first delivery
it is doubtful whether that aim would have
been evident soon enough for a good speech.

We are nearly one-fourth through the sermon before the subject and its treatment is hinted at, and then we must still wait some time until the subject is defined. Nor are we sure that the audience from the circumstances could gather the drift of the speaker until one-third of his speech had been given. This is a trait in Newman not to be imitated. Suspense is often effective and desirable, but to carry it so far in a spoken word where the mind cannot go back and pick up the connexion, is against the practice and teaching of all speakers. There are two other of Newman's sermons given under similar circumstances. *Christ upon the Waters* has many marked points of similarity and deserves to be compared to *The Second Spring* throughout. It is however less compact and less graceful than the latter, but covers practically the same ground. *Order, the Witness and Instrument of Unity*, was delivered a year after at the First Diocesan Synod of Birmingham. It is less picturesque, less musical, less emotional, less exultant than *The Second Spring*. In both of these sermons we are given some clue to the course of the thought yet not definite enough for an ordinary audience. Perhaps it may be urged that the intellectual character of the hearers in these instances renders clearer indications

unnecessary.   There is value in the objection,
but it will be found that in Newman's case
the practice of beginning with a general topic
is almost habitual.

Other principles of Newman's art in sermons may be arrived at by his statements
concerning Cicero.   When Newman was
nearly seventy he wrote: " As to patterns
for imitation the only master of style I have
ever had (which is strange considering the
differences of the language) is Cicero.   I
think I owe a great deal to him and as far as
I know to no one else.   His great mastery of
Latin is shown especially in his clearness."
(*Letters and Correspondence*, II, 427.)

Who would have thought that the disci-
plining which the Latin language and pre-
eminently Cicero, the great moulder of all
modern prose, had given to English, was to
continue on to our day, although English itself seemed to have authors enough to accom-
plish the task?   What are the lessons Newman learnt from Cicero?   Clearness, he
mentions in the words just cited.   Other
qualities may be learned from his essay on
Cicero and from *The Idea of a University*.
In both places when speaking of Cicero as an
orator he lays stress upon qualities which
critics have found in his own works and
which we may presume he derived from his

master. "His copious, majestic, musical flow of language, even if sometimes beyond what the subject-matter demands, is never out of keeping with the occasion or with the speaker." [1] These words which Newman applies to Cicero apply very well to himself. Newman was a musician; he wrote Latin prose; he studied Cicero: and the result of it all was a harmony of style noticed by every reader. "A subtle musical beauty runs elusively through all " Newman's prose. " Not that there is any of the sing-song of pseudo-poetic prose. The cadences are always wide-ranging and delicately shifting, with none of the haughty iteration and feeble sameness of half-metrical works." [2] The harmony of Newman's prose is not obstrusive like Ruskin's, nor always jingling like Macaulay's. In *The Second Spring* a close reader will find him resorting to an inversion or other device to avoid the excessive balance that marks Macaulay, and his use of alliteration and rhythmical clauses and other more palpable devices of harmony is always more sparing and more significant than Ruskin's.

In this *The Second Spring* is characteristic of Newman. Perhaps there is no better example of the haunting melody of Newman's

[1] *Idea of a University*, p. 281.
[2] Gates: *Newman as a Prose-Writer.*

prose and of his indebtedness to Cicero than the variety and smoothness of his sentences. His paragraphs never sputter like the English of the day, and yet for their equable flow he has not at his command the abundant linking that marks his master's style. That he should have been able to attain such variety in an uninflected language like the English is still more remarkable and surely due to his knowledge of Latin prose. The reader who will pick out and place side by side or rather read in close connection the longer periods of *The Second Spring* will find a variety that no other English writer offers and to which he can find a parallel only in Cicero. No purple patches either, but everything woven into the web of his discourse without any startling discrepancy of color or design.

Cicero was copious and clear and was copious in order to be clear. Such is Newman's view: "The perfection of strength is clearness united to brevity; but to this combination Latin is utterly unequal. From the vagueness and uncertainty of meaning which characterizes its separate words, to be perspicuous it must be full." It is not enough for Cicero, Newman says again in the same essay on Cicero, to have barely proved his point; he proceeds to heighten the effect by amplification. "Here he goes (as it were) round and round his object; surveys it in every light; examines it in all its parts; retires and then advances; turns and re-turns it; illustrates, confirms, enforces his view of the question, till at last the hearer feels ashamed of doubting a position which seems built on a foundation so strictly argumentative." Is not that a description of Newman himself? Is not that a detailed view of his own powers, which have made him the greatest master of clear and full exposition our language can boast of? Newman is so copious and so clear that he has been subjected to the same criticism as his model Cicero and he may justly be said to incur the accusation Longfellow urged against a certain sermon, not of being too logical, but of having too much logic. It is that scrupulous care to make his meaning clear which often renders Newman's sermons too intellectual and in that respect inferior models for a speaker. Here he did not imitate Cicero closely enough.

Newman's rather strict ideas about unity in a sermon, which would seem to exclude all but one phase of the subject, was another cause that threw him back upon detailed exposition. The more restricted a writer's subject is, the more he must analyze it, the more he must refine upon the thought if he is to develop the matter to any length. *The Second Spring* displays Newman's powers of exposition but does not manifest the excess which may be found elsewhere, although the opening paragraphs develop the general theme to too great a length.

Newman, says an author, " is the one prose writer of the nineteenth century who achieves a great manner without the least trace of mannerisms." [1]   Here is a trait which all critics agree in ascribing to him and one sufficient in itself to place him among the classicists.   To be free of mannerisms is to be humble enough to suppress individuality and submit to rule.   One cannot, therefore, avoid surprise, seeing an excellent treatise on the style of Cicero,[2] begin with a discussion which showed Newman mastering the rules of classical rhetoric under Whately and end with classifying Newman among the romanticists.   Any classification that couples Newman, who when a boy wrote like Addison and Gibbon and subjected himself to the discipline of Latin, with Carlyle, the apotheosis of the individual and the prince of mannerists, must be absurd on the face of it.   It is equally hard to understand how another can say that " *The Second Spring* marks in litera-

[1] Gwynn: *Masters of English Literature.*
[2] Gates: *Newman as a Prose-Writer.*

ture a moment of the Romantic triumph." [1]
That Newman was touched and influenced by
the Romantic movement cannot be denied,
but a love of Scott's stories and a love of nature which is rather Hebraic than either
Romantic or Classic and is certainly not
Romantic in its chastened sobriety, are rather
doubtful arguments upon which to base a
claim, if the terms Romantic and Classic are
to have any significance whatsoever. The
one argument above all others that clearly
establishes Newman's claim to the term Classic, is the humble suppression of self-asser-
tion and the complete absence of that egotis-
tic conceit which is so marked in nearly all
the great English writers of the nineteenth
century with the exception of Newman.
Whatever decision may be made with regard
to the right classification, this is at any rate
certain: *The Second Spring* is so far characteristic of Newman and his model, Cicero,
as not to be marred with mannerisms.

In the build of his sermons Newman is not
at all Ciceronian, however much he may be
in his sentences and paragraphs. *The Second Spring* is here also characteristic. His
Catholic sermons, at least in their larger outlines, consist of two parts: a law and its application; a law and its exception; a problem

[1] Barry: *Cardinal Newman.*

and its solution; a mystery and its exemplification; and an analogy and its analogue. The very titles of his sermons are often enough to show this: Purity and Love, Nature and Grace, Faith and Private Judgment, Faith and Doubt, Men not Angels, The Priests of the Gospel, Christ upon the Waters, The Second Spring. Newman only at times directly refers to his audience or the place or the occasion; Cicero always does. Newman is impersonal at the outset; Cicero scarcely ever so anywhere. In fact Newman may be said to avoid the classical exordium altogether. He has no division in the usual sense of the term and rarely makes an explicit proposition, except one to which he works up after a long explanation. He likes to begin with a general truth or with a class and a contrast, finding in it some problem to be worked out. There is " a dispensation or state of things which is very strange " or a truth " may strike us with wonder " or as a " difficulty " or inquirers put " a strange question " or " a strange time this may seem " or " I am going to assert a great paradox." Such are the phrases found at the beginning of several sermons in succession. The strangeness seems to stimulate Newman's energy and his marvellous powers of exposition begin to explain away the mystery.

The internal structure of Newman's oratory differs much from the classical whether of Greece or Rome. Demosthenes breaks up his explanation and proof into smaller divisions and follows with the emotional enforcement of his point. He rises and falls like the sea from the quiet of transition and explanation to the stormy crest of emotion. Cicero follows a similar but more conventional plan. He will rise at the end of his introduction and then glide down to his explanation and proofs with varying intensity like rolling ground with wide valleys and slight elevations rising on the horizon into a high elevation. Newman pursues a different course. He explains and confirms and illustrates and gives instances with but slight differences in the level of his style. His paragraphs, it is true, often show differences of level, but in the long run as wholes they maintain nearly the same height. He wings his way with the ease and lightness of a bird and no one can detect any weariness of the pinions that ceaselessly and smoothly cut onward. Then suddenly but not too sharply he soars aloft, not for a long time, but for a glorious flight while it lasts. There is an amplitude to the sentences, a sublimity in the ideas and a height and range and graceful sweep to the feeling. Exclamations, apostrophes, the impassioned language of Scripture, fall upon the ear. Then Newman is not classical, not Romantic, but something nobler, something grander than either, he is Hebraic. He sees with a prophet's eye, feels with a prophet's heart, and in the wider and richer outlook of his imagination feels that he must borrow the prophet's language and end with the prophet's prayer.

To bring *The Second Spring* into the classical mould would require a new arrangement of its paragraphs with some necessary modifications of the language. The two paragraphs at the end, being personal and explanatory of his fitness to speak, would form the exordium. Then there would be a proposition stating that the establishment of the Hierarchy was an exceptional but threatening spring. For the traditional narrative we should have probably the description of the Synod, followed by a proof of the first part of the proposition. Grace had performed a miracle in causing an exception to the usual law of mortality that rules man and all his works. The second part of the proposition would have the nature of a refutation. The dangers of the Protestant outcry would be described and the priests and prelates would be encouraged to meet the possible results, and on that theme, summing up both parts, the speaker would close.

Such an arrangement would be Ciceronian and classical; it would not be characteristic of Newman. No doubt it would destroy the beauty of the sermon. Whether it would impair its utility is a more debatable question. Dr. Barry has stated that Newman was always academic in his sermons and never popular. Thirty years at a university is not the best training for one who would speak to the people. Yet Newman could and did speak to the people when occasion required, as in the *Present Position of Catholics in England.* In the pulpit, however, he remained academic. Such he is in *The Second Spring.* He will not speak of a telescope, but of " a more perfect mechanism than this earth has discovered for surveying the transactions of another globe." His comparisons are but a short remove from the poetic, and when he does take an illustration from the railway in *Christ upon the Waters* he apologizes for its homeliness. Imagine the Apostles apologizing for ploughs or wagons or hens or brooms or the like, which occur in the sermons of the Gospel.

The student of oratory may, therefore, go to Newman's Catholic sermons for clearness, for harmonious and various types of sentences, for orderly paragraphs, for imagination with a wide outlook, for dramatic presentation, for warmth and nobility of feeling and for everything he owes to Latin and Hebrew, but unless the student seek the art of speaking on special occasions when charm rather than popular preaching is looked for, he will not go to Newman for those qualities which were drawn from his University life — the diffuseness of reasoning, the structure of his sermons, the poetic and somewhat fastidious vocabulary, the refined cast of thought, and the other traits which marked him as academic.   In all these qualities, however, both the excellent as well as the less good, *The Second Spring* will be found characteristic and representative of Newman.

The Sermon Notes of John Henry Cardinal Newman have been published subsequent to the writing of most of this chapter. The book supplements our knowledge of Newman's methods, but the material is too scant to establish any definite conclusions. As far, however, as the scant evidence enables us to judge, Newman followed for many years the method we find exemplified in his published Catholic sermons.   The *Notes* are set forth under brief headings which are very often about eleven in number.   The opening

is in most cases styled the Introduction, and
the close once is called the Exhortation and
once Reflection.   True to the principles he
advises in his *Lectures on University Preaching*, Newman has no divisions.   He does not
group his remarks under headings but puts
them down in a logical order.   He has what
the rhetoricians call a disposition, but no division.   His introduction is actual in a few instances only, where there is a special cere-
mony.   On the Anniversary of the Establishment of the Oratory in England, at the
Christmas of 1854, and on two other occasions the sermons referred to persons and
events of the day.   In the application of the
sermons there are, of course, more allusions
to contemporary events.   But the introduction more commonly, as in Newman's other
Catholic sermons, opens with a discussion of
some wonder or mystery or surprise connected with the truth to be discussed, or a
general truth which is to prepare the way for
a particular truth, coming later on in the sermon.   Newman's mind cuts deep.   He takes
no surface view of things.   He is fundamental and gets at the philosophy of every subject.   The analysis of congratulation, and of
love, may be cited as instances of thorough
and perhaps too detailed treatment of a simple idea.   If it is a general law he is ex-

pounding, then he recurs to Scripture for illustration and proof. The *Notes* show Newman to have possessed a wide and ready acquaintance with the Bible, not only in the more common texts but also in new texts or in a new application of the old. At other times his establishment of a general law takes him through history, and we find many instances of that wealth of historical allusions which is found so richly exemplified in the *Essay on Development*. I may refer in this connexion to the sermon "On External Religion" preached at the opening of St. Peter's, Birmingham. After the proof Newman recurs to particular instances and illustrations, and again sacred and profane history yield of their rich stores.

Newman finds his truths exemplified in nature also, either where he shows that a law is true of nature in its widest extent or where he points out the contrast between nature and grace, a topic which seems a favorite one with him. Nature too is made to furnish comparisons. These are often of that delicate beauty of which his sermons give us many examples. He compares the unity of the Church in history to a shadow. "As a shadow may move onwards and presents the same outline over hills and dales, so as time has gone, this one grouping has gone on for eighteen centuries." The dissatisfaction found in sin is likened to drinking salt water or to a receding horizon. Newman's comparisons seemed to depart from their almost poetical delicacy as he advanced in life. At least the *Notes* show him appealing to objects that come more home to man than the aspects of external nature. Sin he likens to an offence against the senses where the least imperfection is destructive: " The sweetest nosegay spoiled by one bad scent of one dead leaf. One drop of bitter in the most pleasant drink. And so of hearing, one discordant note." Again time is " like a railway train, bowling away into darkness." We may call attention here to the five different occasions in which Newman preached on disease as a type of sin.

Despite these popular comparisons and the references to actual events which occur often, the general impression of Newman's preaching left by the *Sermon Notes* confirms Dr. Barry's judgment that Newman was always academic. *Sermon Notes* show that he was more theoretical than practical, that he was excessive in the multiplication and development of his proofs, that he leaned more to dogmatic discussions than moral teaching and more to controversy than to positive exposition. The delicacy of his comparisons from nature is paralleled by the subtlety of his analogies, and by the learnedness of his allusions. His wonderful mind circled out into wide arcs and touched remote but concentric ideas which went beyond the span of ordinary individuals. He saw truths in aspects new and original but too elusive for the running world. Newman has always been known to be sensitive to logical accuracy. This trait receives confirmation in *Sermon Notes*. On several occasions he gives substitute arrangements of the same set of notes, and in each case he seeks the logical arrangement usual with him but not that which makes a sermon intelligible at once and throughout. Newman begins afar at some distant truth and finally works down to the matter in hand. It is fascinating to study this where one has all the links of thought before him on the printed page, but it is not the way to instant understanding on the part of the listeners, who have limited powers of comprehension and no means of backward reference except an untrained memory.

The best part of Newman's preaching, the part that furnishes the largest portion of those eloquent extracts with which constant citations have made us familiar, finds unhappily no illustration in *Sermon Notes*. As has already been stated, the emotional appeal is merely noted in a word. The proofs we could get elsewhere, but it is an irreparable loss to the pulpit that the wonderful conclusions to all these sermons were never written down in full. The few we have in the published Catholic sermons make regrets all the more bitter.

VIII

PARDOW AND THE POPULAR STYLE

VIII

PARDOW AND THE POPULAR STYLE

FATHER PARDOW'S vocation was that of a preacher. It might be said that he lived for preaching. How early in life this idea took possession of him may not perhaps be easily determined. His weak health during his first years as a religious may have disposed him to turn his thoughts to the pulpit if he had not already done so. The years devoted to teaching by the young Jesuit before priesthood were not spent by Father Pardow in the class-room. His health did not permit him to teach. This exclusion would naturally turn his zealous energy toward another outlet. The impossibility of continued application did not encourage in him the hope of being a teacher or a writer. So he would be a preacher. He read many hours a day during that time and, as he said, was especially fond of history, probably the history of the Church, which fostered, no doubt, his turn for controversy on historical subjects.

Wherever or whenever he conceived the idea of occupying the pulpit, certain it is that every detail of his life was influenced by it. He took walks daily and daily exercised his lungs with deep breathing. His cold-water bath before retiring was especially directed, as he admitted, to keep from colds and so preserve his voice from hoarseness. From the very first he welcomed all criticism and wrote down the most minute details concerning voice, gesture, and language, which his

---

The Rev. William O'Brien Pardow, S.J., was born in New York City, 13 June, 1847, was graduated from St. Francis Xavier's College in the same city in 1864, and entered the Society of Jesus, on August 31 of that year. He afterwards was Rector of his Alma Mater, was Provincial of the Maryland-New York Province of his order, acted in various other offices of responsibility and trust, and at the time of his death was superior and pastor of the Church of St. Ignatius Loyola in New York City. His chief work was that of preaching and giving retreats which he carried on for thirty years in all parts of the United States and Canada. He died 23 January, 1909.

For complete details, see the excellent life, *William Pardow of the Company of Jesus,* Justine Ward, Longmans, Green & Co. The chapter on Father Pardow's preaching is one of the best in the book and should be read by all students of eloquence.

critics pointed out to him. The practice itself is characteristic of the man, and his
frankness in facing these faults and his per-
sistence in working at their removal are worthy of note. For twenty-five years he kept
up this practice, noting failures to prevent
their recurrence and successes to ensure their
repetition. Nothing shows so clearly Father
Pardow's complete devotion to preaching
than this collection of favorable and unfavor-
able criticisms.

The principal work of his life was done in
retreats and sermons, and his theory and
practice were to accept all possible invita-
tions to speak. His apostolic ardor in this
line and his resolute courage, which prompted
him from the beginning never to bring a note
into the pulpit, never to write a sermon,
found it hard to make allowances for others
who did not have this confidence. He was
good enough to think others capable of doing
what he did. The same enthusiasm for the
spoken word led him, when in the office of
Instructor of the Tertians, as it is called, he
explained the constitutions of his order, to
dwell enthusiastically on the Society's work in
preaching. He used to point with great satisfaction to the fact that St. Ignatius first intended his order for the missions and that
teaching was forced upon him by circum-

stances.   One reason, too, we may believe,
why Father Pardow showed a marked liking
for St. Francis Xavier was the fact that the
professor of Paris became a preacher and the
Apostle of the Indies.

Scarcely for a moment of the day did
Father Pardow forget that he was a
preacher.   He was always preparing for his
next sermon.   Books were read with that
purpose in view; papers and magazines were
made to yield up clippings to be filed away
for future use.   His walks furnished him
with illustrations and examples to clarify an
idea or enforce a point.   In Washington, it
is said, he went into a store to examine a
cash-register in order to illustrate from its
workings the practice of the examination of
conscience.   When going to Woodstock,
Md., once to give a retreat, he rode part
way on the trolley-car.   He noticed that the
lights burned brighter when the car stopped.
That fact suggested to him, as he explained
to one who was asking him about the art of
illustration, that the grace of God may be displayed in men's lives by giving them power,
even if they are in desolation.   A decrease of
sensible devotion would not argue a lessening
of God's grace but a diverting of its energy
to other work.   The young Jesuit who
sought information and was trying to learn

how to make comparisons, sorrowfully admitted that he never would have thought of all that or anything like it as the incandescent lamps faded and flared. His thoughts had not one direction as Father Pardow's had. Every place Father Pardow visited furnished him with new material to give fresh treatment to old truths. The Niagara Falls, California and the long ride there, a voyage to Jamaica, a journey to Rome, all were pressed into service in sermons and retreats.

He liked to make his sermon titles striking. This practice hurt him perhaps a little in the appreciation of conservative judges and conveyed the impression to some who drew their conclusions often from these startling head-lines, that his preaching was sensational. He was indeed picturesque and very modern in his illustrations, but that his language was undignified or low is not at all true. In the enthusiasm of the moment, in order "to point a point," as he frequently exhorted himself to do in his notes, he was led to use words which he was himself the first to condemn. In his long career as a public speaker there are few lapses from good taste to be recorded. In the two dozen or more sermons which survive and which were taken down in shorthand, there is nothing

which could be so characterized.   The vocabulary has no slang.

His sermons were not in the least what
would be called literary in the choice of
words or turn of sentences.   A very rare instance in which he departed from his custom
in this matter occurred at the end of a retreat
where in explaining the apparition of Jesus
at early morning to the disappointed disciples, he alluded to the rising sun of the new
day.   One who had often heard him preach
remarked with surprise at a phrase of two
savoring of impassioned prose.   Father Pardow was essentially a preacher, a talker.
He was simple, direct, and preëminently
clear.   You might disagree with his position
or conclusions; you could not mistake them.
His thoughts disengaged themselves from all
unessential or superfluous details and stood
out in bold relief.   He " pointed his points."
The same quality characterized his delivery.
He was distinct almost to a fault and yet re-
proached himself if a single person missed
a single word.   Distinct articulation was
helped by correct and perfect emphasis.   A
professor of elocution, on hearing one of his
sermons, remarked with enthusiasm on the
clear-cut prominence of the right words.

He was sensitive to the slightest inatten-
tion and watched his audience as a doctor

would a patient. It was this desire to hold his hearers that may have led him to use phrases which conservative critics viewed with displeasure. He was always in touch with his audience, congratulated them on their attention, relieved the strain by a humorous description, arrested and fascinated wandering thoughts with an illustration from sources familiar to all and went home to their hearts with vivid sketches of personal experience.

He was better at exposition than argumentation and more skilled in argumentation than in appeals to emotions, at least of the tenderer kind. The range of subjects which he touched upon was not wide or varied but it embraced within its compass the most vital topics of the day, the Bible, the Church, education, divorce. These were his great subjects. He had no profound views or new theories to expound. He was not a great theologian or philosopher. He was content to move in a lower circle. He loved the practical art of popularizing. He had a clear grasp of the few essential truths connected with his favorite topics, and he had the faculty of driving them home and making them stick. It has been the experience of many to remember Father Pardow's sermons longer than those of any one else.

It is more than twenty-five years ago since
the writer first heard Father Pardow in a retreat to the students of Fordham College.
His thin frame, his short, incisive gestures,
his earnest efforts to be distinct, but most of
all his flashes of humor and his power of exciting fear, stand out distinctly in the memory
to this day. The two last points go back to
a prime quality in Father Pardow's preaching, his force of imagination. Writers and
speakers are recommended to describe with
their eye on the scene. Father Pardow's
lively imagination not only saw the scene but
was an actor in it and dramatized it for his
listeners. His famous sermon on the General Judgment was a signal instance of his
power in this regard. The old college chapel
at Fordham became the stage of that tremendous tragedy. The students took their
places, received their sentences and shivered
with horror at the arming of the great Judge
and the piteous appeal of the speaker to Him
not to enclose His Heart in a breast-plate of
steel. The words of Wisdom (5:18 ff)
were paraphrased, enacted with a vividness
which drew from all a sigh of relief as the
preacher reassured his audience, what his
graphic language had made them forget, that
it was but a rehearsal after all.

The same imaginative powers helped his

faculty of illustration.   He never used a trite
comparison in a trite way.   He saw distinctly
and vividly, as if it was present, what he used
for comparison; more than that, as far as
such a thing could be, he became for the time
being the object serving for illustration.
You could detect it in his eye, feel it in his
voice, and witness it in his gesture.   For this
reason his exposition of passages of Scripture
took on a special vividness and an unhackneyed fulness of detail.   The Gospel story
was enacted anew.   The Gospel parables
and mysteries disclosed countless lessons and
novel applications, which delighted the listeners, though surprising the matter-of-fact
critic.   One thought of St. John Chrysostom,
St. Augustine, Pope St. Gregory, rather than
of the scientific expositors of more recent
times.   Father Pardow's exposition was
popular and practical and more inclined to
find figurative lessons in the pall-bearers of
the Widow of Nain's son than to furnish a
small-sized gazetteer for the mother's town.
His imagination reveled in foundations of·
rock and sand, in discoveries of fruit and
leaves and the varying proportions of these
which every soul might be considered to
have, and he discussed with ingenious fulness
where the rain-storms might occur in daily
life and what periods of the day grew more

leaves and what reared fruits for the Gardener's blessing.   Some who heard him on retreats considered him a great Scripture scholar; others, hearing fanciful interpretations, thought little of his knowledge of the Bible.   He used to tell of a bishop who characterized his work as displaying a diligent use of the concordance.   Both sets of critics missed the point.   Father Pardow took the Bible as a book to be taught, not one to write encyclopedias about.   He had mastered its lessons in daily meditation and strove to convey that lesson to others.   The revelation of Holy Writ was more to him than its antiquities.   His exegesis was occasionally at fault; his fancy ran riot at times, but he taught his listeners how to contemplate and brought them close to Christ, our Lord.   He was in that sense patristic and medieval.

The lighter side of Father Pardow's preaching found its source also to some extent in his powers of imagination.   He was a most interesting speaker.   It is a test to speak to a body of priests four or five times a day for thirty days and not bore them. This test was successfully met by Father Pardow, year after year, when he conducted the Spiritual Exercises of St. Ignatius for thirty days, and a large factor in this success was his saving sense of humor.   A favorite phrase of his was: it is better to laugh than to sleep, and when his watchful eye detected any weariness in his hearers, he immediately enlivened his words by something in a lighter vein. His imagination supplied him with an incongruous detail or his dramatic powers suggested a characterization of some person or scene, verging upon caricature, and with the relief of a smile the weariness of prolonged seriousness passed away.

To the same faculty of imaginative realization may be ascribed Father Pardow's ability to satirize. The wide difference between resolution and performance was something which he often described in withering irony. Perhaps his own inflexible determination and sincerity kept him from making the allowances he might for the weakness of human nature. It was this trait in his character which contributed to make the confessional especially onerous. He found it hard to conceive that a sincere purpose of amendment is not inconsistent with future relapses. He was somewhat scrupulous on the point and was inclined to question the firmness of the penitent's resolution, and so it was that this sad inconsistency of our nature became the target for his irony. The writer remembers two instances among others where this faculty of irony was strongly displayed. In one

case St. Peter's boast and his unhappy sleep
were depicted in a way hard to forget.   It
was a retreat, where Father Pardow's powers
of impersonation had greater scope.   The
apostle's very attitude was taken off as he
murmured in sleepy tones: "Wake me up
when you want me to die."   On another occasion when giving the Contemplation on the
Love of God at the close of an eight days'
retreat, the pitiless exposure of our essential
smallness and meanness was simply terrible.
The impression was profound.   It may have
been discouraging to some, but to others the
probing disclosure of their real selves, like
the surgeon's knife, was humiliating but
profitable.   On that occasion, one, at least,
found it hard to sleep during the night, just
as at another time many of the Georgetown
students after one of his sermons refused to
go to bed until they had seen their Father
Confessor and relieved their consciences.
Father Pardow had made eternal truths present and effective by vivid presentation, and
sleep became a menace to students of careless
conscience.

In the structure of his sermons he rarely
followed the conventional arrangement of
matter which the great French preachers
elaborated.   Here, too, he was patristic.
His style was more akin to the homilies of

Chrysostom and St. Augustine than to the fixed divisions and methodical development of a Bourdaloue. He admired and appreciated such preaching and possessed the requisite powers of analysis to carry through such a sermon, but he claimed to have satisfied himself by actual observation that such a style of preaching might appeal to himself but left the congregations, as he witnessed, passive. How far these observations are correct, and whether passive and dull listeners are necessarily to be found where the sermon is methodical, does not concern us here; at all events, Father Pardow never followed that style. His sermons, in most cases, did not form a strict unit. Rather they gave the impression of a series of thoughts, developed through several paragraphs and presenting a central topic from various points of view. It might be said that at his best he produced a unity of impression, though lacking in perfect unity of expression. You went away, not with one proposition explained, established, defended against all objections and driven home by vigorous enforcement. You had rather a number of such truths, some of which remained with you a long time and all helped to lift your mind to higher ideals and braced you for vigorous exertion. In his retreats this effect

was still more evident.   His explanations of
the mysteries did not divide logically and
group themselves under heads.   He was essentially homiletic here, presenting the various phases of the Gospel record in succession.

Father Pardow lacked many of the natural gifts we look for in a great orator.
His presence was not commanding; his voice
was not rich or musical; his action was vigorous but somewhat stiff and angular.   One
would say, " What a strong speaker! " not,
" What a graceful speaker! "   Indeed, it
can be truly said that he succeeded in spite of
difficulties of mind and body which would
have deterred or wearied a less determined
character.   Most people knew Father Pardow through his appearance in public, and it
can be safely said that the estimation of him
formed in that way gave a true picture of the
man.   The best qualities of his sermons
were the true expression of his daily life and
a reflection of his religious experiences.   His
very careful distinctness, his selection and
enunciation and repetition of strong and
favorite phrases, were not qualities put on in
the pulpit.   All his prayers had these qualities and at Mass his measured distinctness of
tone was quite noticeable.   Even if there
was only the acolyte present, he wished him,
as he said, to be able to follow..   It is known

that for a whole year he took the words of
the Mass for his daily meditation.

The Spiritual Exercises of St. Ignatius,
which entered so largely into his life, calls
for that loving study of the force of words.
The methods of prayer there explained are
very much concerned with dwelling on the
meaning of words. The same *Exercises*
would develop, if not initiate, the habit of
illustrating. Comparisons figure prominently in the meditations, and the making of
them is even inculcated as part of the Second
Method of Prayer. There, it may have
been, that Father Pardow began or strength-
ened the habit of looking for illustrations
which figured so prominently in his sermons
and was exemplified in everything he read
and commented upon. The handling of
Scripture in the living and practical way
which characterized Father Pardow was also
encouraged, if not actually originated, by
St. Ignatius's method of contemplation.
Through the practice of that method he was
brought into touch with the traditional contemplation of the Church, exemplified especially by St. Bonaventure, whose ways in
prayer he spoke of as being exactly those of
St. Ignatius in many of his exercises and
most of all in the Nativity.

That Father Pardow in the pulpit did not

appeal to all is not remarkable. Very few
preachers do.   It is remarkable that he appealed to so wide a circle of hearers for so
many years., His name attracted crowds
wherever he was announced to speak. He
never failed to draw and draw largely. The
Confessional is a good gauge of the effectiveness of sermons and Father Pardow's sermons successfully stood that test. Those
who were least in sympathy with his style
bore cheerful witness of the fruitfulness of
his words.

No analysis of word or gesture or study
of style will disclose the secret of Father
Pardow's admitted success as a preacher.
Emphasis, distinctness, comparisons, telling
epigrams, were but means and instruments.
It was the man, the religious, the saintly
character, which attracted and persuaded.
His appearance, his life, his intense convic-
tions, his palpable sincerity, were the factors
in his preaching which were most effective.
All else was little, however helpful or even
necessary. He perfected himself in the ac-
cessories of eloquence, but never sought
them for themselves. If the idea ever suggested itself to him that this or that means
or style would put him in or out of the category of orators, he would have dismissed the
thought as frivolous and would have depre-

cated any discussion of such topics as academic. Father Pardow saved souls by preaching God's word as best he knew how. Any further classification is unprofitable theorizing.

IX
INTEREST FROM ANTAGONISM

IX

INTEREST FROM ANTAGONISM

THE best speech is a duel. The orator has before him in reality or in imagination an antagonist with whom he grapples. Demosthenes, who learned the art from his teacher, Isæus, was the prince of oratorical duellists. He never lets slip from him his audience or his antagonist. Drop Æschines from the Crown speech and you may make of it a brief history of a certain period of Greece, but you make it a lifeless corpse. Cicero felt that his audiences called for less intensity of concentration upon him and he indulged in digressions and discussions of general topics that Demosthenes would dismiss in a sentence or phrase, but Cicero is too great a writer to be summed up in a formula. He too felt the spell of an antagonist and knew how to respond to it. Harmony, balance, the prolonged pomp of periods are not the complete description of Rome's great orator. Mark him when he meets an antagonist. He quickly drops the

143

brilliancy and pomp and resorts to the parry
and thrust, with as much skill as his Athenian rival.   His refutations are quite the opposite to what passes usually for Ciceronian.
The first part of his speech for Archias is
altogether unlike the latter part. His
speech for Ligarius, his Philippics might be
called un-Ciceronian, they are so modern.
The truth is most people remember Cicero
by some opening periods rather than by the
passages and speeches where he faces and
fights an antagonist.

The value of an antagonist to bring a
speech out of the vagueness of an essay into
the sharp definiteness of a debate is very well
illustrated in the speeches of Mr. Bryan.
From the Biographical Sketch, written by his
wife, which forms an introduction to the volumes, we learn that Mr. Bryan began early
to contest for prizes.   In fact it was only on
his fourth attempt that he succeeded in get-
ting into first place.   Besides taking part in
these literary contests, he was diligent in debate.   Debate was his favorite means in his
political campaigns.   His first and most successful campaign for Congress was marked
by eleven debates with his opponent.   His
astonishing success in a normally Republican
district must have been due in no small measure to these debates.   His opponents were

induced to enter into debates on other occasions but, taught no doubt by experience, the meetings were fewer. Mr. Bryan has the greatest respect for debating. In the latest speech published in these volumes and in some respects the most interesting, he treats of Lincoln as an orator. The speech derives its interest not from the subject only but because its gives us Mr. Bryan's ideal of an orator and, as we should naturally expect, the traits which appeal to him in Lincoln are principally the traits we find in himself. Lincoln's debates with Douglas are properly emphasized by Mr. Bryan, as the first step to the presidency. " No other American President has ever so clearly owed his elevation to his oratory."

The speeches of Mr. Bryan afford an opportunity to exemplify and test the effects of the principle of antagonism in oratory. They fall short, even in their best portions, of the fiery directness of Wendell Phillips, who fairly revelled in antagonism and seemed even to seek it in the way he flew in the face of all lessons of rhetoric and goaded his audience into fury against him in the very beginning of his speech, only to triumph the more surely at the close. But although Mr. Bryan is not as antagonistic as Phillips, yet his words and ideas respond to the thrill of antagonism.   The examples of grappling are all the more striking by contrast with speeches of his where there is little or no such directness and intensity.

Mr. Bryan had courage to print his valedictory speech, given at graduation. It is decidedly sophomoric. There is no opponent in sight anywhere. The subject is Character, and the treatment is just as vague. No one could by any possibility disagree with the usual collection of platitudes ending up in the stream of tears customary on such occasions. The speech is no better than hundreds such which are heard every year. Complimentary speeches at banquets are not antagonistic. One such, entitled, " Radical and Conservative," is found in this collection. It follows the usual formula; a modest disclaimer of praise, a witticism at the expense of the presiding officer, a discussion of some general truth, closing with roseate views of the future. Mr. Bryan was then among Japanese in Japan, and there was no place for antagonism at a complimentary banquet.

These and other speeches have parts which glow, but rarely burst into flames, or if they flare with the brightness of sheet-lightning, they fail to condense into the quivering lines that have the flash of death in their leap.

The sting of rivalry is needed to bring ideas into sharp focus, and the heart to fever. Then thoughts are too insistent for utterance to be even winged; they explode into swift bullets. There is the enemy with his eyes upon yours, and language itself cannot be calm. It breaks up into questions and exclamations and brief, pointed phrases. It would become sword-points to pierce the rival. The retort, the sharp contrasts, the scornful reechoing of an opponent's phrase, above all the dilemma where the oratorical duellist grapples with both hands, these are the characteristics of the famous battles of the brain; these may be found in Mr. Bryan's best speeches in this collection.

Many parts of the speech on the Tariff have this quality. Such too are some shorter refutations, as " The Omnivorous West," " Dreamers " and that address called " Commerce," which was given on the historic occasion when a short while before election Mr. Bryan and Mr. Taft met at the same banquet in Chicago. The antagonism is suppressed by politeness, but it tingles there nevertheless. Better examples still are found in " The Trust Question," " Imperialism," " Naboth's Vineyard." In these the elocutionist will find that fiery selection he delights in or he will turn to " America's Mission," which for its length has perhaps the most fire and blood of any of the speeches. Compare the epigrams and historical examples and contrasts in this speech with the things which pass for such in the speech on " Character." The latter are warmed over from books; the former are the hot coinage of the heart.

Yet all things considered, although its famous triumph prejudices one in its favor, the well-known speech at the Chicago Convention of 1896 should be noted as perhaps the crowning instance of the power of antagonism. The best that can be said of it is that it showed the speaker worthy of the effect it helped to produce and drew from his enemies the retort of abuse and misrepresentation, tacit acknowledgments of its power. We venture this criticism and believe it to be true even if the cause Mr. Bryan defended were shown to be wrong. It was not so believed to be then and Mr. Bryan at the time was sincere in defending the cause of silver and shown to be masterful in carrying the wavering convention with him. The fight for silver had been long waged and silver and gold delegates sat in convention with the tense antagonism of drawn battle lines. The following passage should soften any heart except one of gold:

Ah, my friends, we say not one word against those who live upon the Atlantic Coast, but the hardy pioneers who have braved all the dangers of the wilderness, who have made the desert to blossom as the rose — the pioneers away out there (pointing to the west), who rear their children near to Nature's heart, where they can mingle their voices with the voices of the birds, out there where they have erected schoolhouses for the education of their young, churches where they praise their Creator, and cemeteries where rest the ashes of their dead — these people, we say, are as deserving of the consideration of our party as any people in this country. It is for these that we speak. We do not come as aggressors. Our war is not a war of conquest; we are fighting in defense of our homes, our families and posterity. We have petitioned and our petitions have been scorned; we have entreated, and our entreaties have been disregarded; we have begged, and they have mocked when our calamity came. We beg no longer; we entreat no more; we petition no more. We defy them.

There are many splendid passages of contrast in these volumes; in " America's Mission," between Anglo-Saxon and American civilization; in " Imperialism," between Republicans now and formerly, between the policy of imperialism and monarchy; in " The Trust Question," between monopoly and competition and between law and conscience. Such lively contrasts seem to transfer the spirit of antagonism into the body of the speech.

For the scornful echoing of a passage in vigorous refutation we may refer to "The Trust Question," where a statement of Mr. Taft accusing Mr. Bryan of extirpating and destroying the entire business in order to stamp out the evils, is refuted. "Extirpate and destroy" echoes through a long refutation like Antony's "honorable men." The same speech gives examples of the dilemma and the retort, sharp weapons of antagonistic speeches.

We feel that to study Mr. Bryan's speeches in this way is to do them an injustice; because many of his fine lectures are passed over without a word and because even in the matter of style only a partial view is given. Besides Mr. Bryan will be impatient to be treated in this fashion. It may give people the notion that he strives for the graces of style, which he never seems to do. His doctrine and teaching is supreme for him, as it is for every orator, and there is scarcely a question of public life before the country during the past quarter of a century which is not discussed clearly and convincingly in Mr. Bryan's volumes. No style would be of avail without the solidity of true teaching. Yet on the other hand true teaching is shorn of much of its strength without strong and vigorous presentation, and some of Mr. Bryan's speeches deserve to live even after the questions they answer are antiquated.

The effect of antagonism might have been far better illustrated from the classic orators of Greece and Rome or from Fox and Chatham among the English or from any of the Irish orators.   In comparison with those mighty duellists Bryan's strongest passages are weak and ineffective.   But the text books of oratory have made us more or less familiar with these masterpieces of antagonistic oratory, and there is some novelty at least in contemporary illustrations of a distinctive oratorical trait, which has ever riveted the attention of mankind and still continues to number its victories of interest.

X

MACAULAY AND "JOURNALESE"

X

MACAULAY AND "JOURNALESE"

LITERATURE is much concerned and worried about its immortality. Most of the poets of antiquity prophesied that they would never die and those whose prophecies have come down to us have succeeded so far in avoiding the tomb of forgetfulness. How many other poetical prophets have perished with their undying visions we have no means of knowing. Most of the admirers of literature today are busy indulging in like prophecies of immortality for their own particular literary idol. Modern writers are too sophisticated to predict their own undying fame; they leave that work to their critics.

Journalism does not resemble literature in this respect. Journalism is glad to live for the day; literature wishes to live forever. Even the life of a day is more than journalism ambitions. An hour's, a minute's, existence will do. The actor is happy to have reached once over the footlights and awakened one burst of applause. The paragrapher is happy if he arrests the commuter's attention at the first line of his paragraph and then holds him to the last line. The journalist has many difficulties to contend with. He must catch his reader's fickle attention amidst a thousand topics of interesting news, amidst another thousand or more thoughts of coming business engagements or past experiences, amidst many more distractions of cars, scenes and passengers. If the journalist is not successful with such a reader, he will not enjoy the immortality of a second, and his paragraph will find its way to the floor of the car, unread by the distracted commuter.

The news column attracts by its contents if they have been well selected. Every day the newspaper begins or continues some exciting story. Facts usually are interesting; facts daily presented in serial form whet the curiosity to see the story's end. It is not in the news column that journalism must struggle for existence, but rather on the editorial page, in special articles, wherever the subject has no novelty or interest of its own or where readers are indifferent. There journalism must use a new language. There is the field of " journalese."

What are the methods of " journalese "? Who are its masters? The first question first. There is only one sin in "journalese" and that is dullness. Flash at once and then sparkle on forever. You may be only brilliant paste; you are lost if you are an uncut gem. You must flame even if you have not fire. Better be a blind particle of momentarily incandescent flint than an arsenal of unignited explosives. That is why introductions are obsolete in "journalese." Exordiums belong to the paleontological period of literature when men traveled in ox-carts. "Journalese" begins; it does not introduce itself. "Journalese" subsists upon the sparest diet of conjunctions so far known in the history of languages. Mr. Jingle of Pickwick still leads "journalese" by a few lengths. "Albeit," "notwithstanding," "nevertheless," these have gone. "Consequently," "however," "therefore," are still struggling hard for existence. "And," "but," "then," are yet staple diet of the "journalese" menu, but no one knows how long they will last. Rhetoricians tell young writers to bury their connectives in the sentence, rather than commence with them. Wise rhetoricians! You are beginning to surmise what "journalese" has long understood. To ask a reader to travel across the immense logical space indicated by a "notwithstanding," is as fatuous as to invite him

to take a local from New York to Chicago.
The journalist avoids what Austin Dobson
calls " a starched procession of ifs and buts."

Macaulay, of all English writers, contributed most to the making of the language of
the journalist. Macaulay gave swiftness to
the English language. Anything which
called upon the mind to halt, to reflect on
what had gone before, was discarded as far
as could be by Macaulay. His clearness, his
straightforward assertions, his easy philosophy which he browbeats the reader into taking as robust common sense, these are some
of the qualities of Macaulay's thought which
made him one of the founders of " journalese." But his expression or his style, in a
narrow sense, entitles him with more justice
to the name of founder. No style will
sparkle without an epigram. Epigrams ac-
celerate the reader's pace. They are wisdom
in capsules and may be bolted. Macaulay is
epigrammatic. Macaulay's antithetical balance is another help to speed. Each side of
the antithesis gives rapidity to the progress
of the thought. Macaulay, again, dispenses
with pronouns and so gives speed to his
thought. To be forced to recall what " it,"
" this," " that," refer to halts the reader.
Repeat the noun, and the mind leaps ahead.
The student anxious to take a brief course in

" journalese " may be safely recommended to Macaulay.

Take some examples at random from Macaulay's essay on Barere: " A man who has never been within the tropics does not know what a thunderstorm means; a man who has never looked on Niagara has but a faint idea of a cataract; and he who has not read Barere's memoirs may be said not to know what it is to lie." " It would be as unreasonable to expect him to remember all the wretches whom he slew as all the pinches of snuff he took. But, though Barere murdered many hundreds of human beings, he murdered only one queen." " Heredity monarchy may be, and we believe it is, a very useful institution in a country like France. And masts are very useful parts of a ship. But, if the ship is on her beam-ends, it may be necessary to cut the masts away." Passages like these show that Macaulay has the smartness and swiftness we associate with so-called " journalese." Macaulay's style is light-footed. Macaulay has fitted Mercury's wings to his feet and keeps the mind scurrying after his flying thoughts.

What is his secret? It may be simply expressed in the old phrase: Make all your geese swans. The number of truths in this world which can be stated with absolute, unqualified directness is small. Most of these truths are published in the beginning of geometry and a few other kindred books and are called axioms. Macaulay made all truths axiomatic. By the simple omission of all qualifications, he stripped his ideas of every incumbrance and sent them speeding on without the handicap of the many reservations with which laborious thinkers weight their logic. Mr. Henry James will shade and tint a thought with endless touches until he has brought his picture to accuracy and his reader to despair. Mr. Saintsbury will inject parentheses wherever he thinks the thought needs modification until he jolts every notion out of your head. Macaulay scorns all fine distinctions, dashes down everything in black and white, gracefully hurdles parenthetical exceptions and is rapid and journalistic. There are but two classes of ideas: Other things and swans. Every English school boy knows it, or nobody knows it.

The advantages of this contribution to journalism, made by Macaulay, are obvious. The inconveniences are not always so fully grasped. The journalist who by fixing his attention exclusively on a few white feathers and on a vague impression of a winged creature has succeeded in transforming a certain goose into a swan, may escape detection because the reader will not have yesterday's or to-morrow's contribution of the same journalist before him. But if the reader should compare and find that by an identical process of concentrating undivided attention on the goose's hissing, the bird has become a snake, or by an exclusive study of the clay on its feet, it has been built upon into a heap of mud, he may admire the lightning changes of his rapid paragrapher, but will not be enthusiastic over his consistency and logic. The journalist is interesting, is stimulating, but if he will follow Macaulay in roundly asserting every truth in an unqualified fashion, he will come to some grief when he gathers his paragraphs into a book. His readers will be exhilarated, but will no doubt be bewildered to find worry wrecking the universe on one page and duty performing the same tremendous feat on another page.

XI
LITERARY AGILITY

XI

LITERARY AGILITY

A NECESSARY element of cleverness is
rapidity. You may be a genius, but if
you are slow you will not be clever. Wit and
cleverness are near of kin, and everyone expects wit to flash like lightning, though humor
may come with the leisure of the dawn. Remember the best, that is, the worst, punster
you have ever met, and recall how fast his
mind, or at least his memory, worked! He
scurried in thought through a multitude of
similar sounds, rejecting them one after another until he lit upon the one which he in-
flicted upon his hearers. They, alas, prayed
for a more complete rejection.

The clever writer must play with ideas as
the punster plays with sounds. You think
daggers and swords are heavy things which
you must handle gingerly. Then along
comes a juggler and makes daggers leap up
as lightly and brightly as playing fountains,
while swords wing their careless flights hither
and thither at their own sweet will. A clever

writer must have a like dexterity with words and ideas. From history and literature, from the sciences and arts, from all lands and sea and sky, from the varied experiences of life, a thousand thoughts must come speeding and a thousand others stand and wait.

The Greek sophists were the first clever literary men we know of. They were the handy speech-makers of antiquity. They could make the worst reason appear the best, and from that day to this it will be found that cleverness is most displayed in manipulating contrasts and mastering contraries. Take Cicero. He is famously clever and deserves his fame especially for proving his case by the objections brought against it. Take Plutarch's " Lives " in parallel contrasts and likenesses, a clever device, cleverly carried out and the model of countless imitations. Take the medieval sophist, the scholastic philosopher, mentioned by Newman, who agreed to defend the opposite side of a question just brilliantly proved by him. Recall Abelard's famous book of " Yea and Nay." There is again, to pass over other instances, the case of Macaulay. He is accused of preserving the balance of an antithetical sentence at the expense of truth. Doubtless he unwittingly did so at times, as his agile mind leaped from clause to clause, matching idea

with idea, flashing bright thoughts on this
side and that, clearing with easy and disdain-
ful flight wide stretches of history or geog-
raphy, and even wider stretches of logic.

To make everything seem alike where ordinary persons see differences is a manifestation
of cleverness. It is a favorite practice with
novelists to find in one scene or one character
only one trait exemplified, and in the imaginative world, created by story-writers, such
leveling may be permitted however improb-
able the results must at times appear. A
master like Dickens uses this means with
great effect to make the reader's flesh creep
at a scene of pervading gloom, or, on the
other hand, and even more successfully, to
make the reader chuckle with delight at a reiterated grotesque feature or at some quality
ironically impressed on him by grave repetitions. The "solidity" of everything in
Podsnap's dining-room is an instance in point.
You will find it an exhilarating gymnastic of
the mind to make everything in a person or
place illustrate one point. If you wish to see
how clever you are, take an adjective and
carry it down a street or all over a person,
making every particular part stand and deliver your adjective. Carry that off well and
you may class yourself with so clever a writer
as James Douglas, who in his book " The

Man in the Pulpit " transfers the methods of
Dickens to the prose of fact, with vivacity
and dash, but with some straining of reality.
Mr. Douglas is a " journalese " critic, ad-
dicted perhaps to overseasoning in trying to
be clever.   Note this typical passage :

> Canon Barker's smile is a sermon and his sermon
> is a smile.   As he expounds the religion of peace,
> the peace of religion, you realize that his face is
> carved out of joyous quietude.   Its smooth surfaces
> are genial, untormented.   The small eyes twinkle
> contentment.   The nose juts out with jovial hilar-
> ity.   Every gesture is an incitement to a cheerful
> acceptance of life.   The strained mouth, drawn
> tight as a bow-string, seems to battle with an inner
> tide of laughter that surges for relief.   The man is
> an incarnation of optimism.

One of the most exhilarating phases of
Mr. Chesterton's cleverness is concerned with
contrasts and contradictories.   His agility is
shown in being able to unite the most incongruous ideas.   Perhaps the most remarkable
instance of this power is found in the story
called " The Honor of Israel Gow."   The
whole book, " The Innocence of Father
Brown," in which a Catholic priest is made
to outrival Sherlock Holmes, displays the
cleverness of contradictories, but the particular story about Israel Gow, which is a hu-

morous satire on thrift, subtly suggested by
the Scotch-Hebrew name, makes Sherlock
Holmes, when compared with Father Brown,
seem a veritable pygmy in the art of being
clever.   This reverend detective gives off-
hand several theories to weave into harmony
a number of most extraordinarily and gro-
tesquely diverse items.   Cleverness could
scarcely be more agile; but the final solution
remains still more clever, and many other
solutions, we doubt not, were possible to so
supple a mind.

Yet, after all, Mr. Chesterton's stories are
his own inventions, which it is not surprising
that he should be able to manipulate at pleasure.   He is still more agile when he goes farther than harmonizing the seemingly incongruous and shows you that truth is the exact
contradictory of what you have hitherto
thought.   The wise are alone foolish; the
insane, the only sane; the miserable are
wildly hilarious; the laughing are bathed in
tears; the people who live in glass houses
should throw stones and no one else — such
as these are the truths which come easy to
Mr. Chesterton's swiftly-working brain.

Consider a passage like the following:
Wiseacres are always telling us that two and
two make four.   Yet if you consider, you
will find there is more falsity than truth in

that particular bit of hoary but heretical
mathematics.   An equation may be an eva-
sion, and the prevaricating powers of figures,
whether as statistics or as plain unadorned
numerals, call for no special remark.   " Two
and two make four."   In the case of Kil-
kenny cats what do they make?   Nothing of
the kind.   What of married couples?   Two
and two made two until Reno made us un-
learn our matrimonial mathematics.   Take
your equation, Messieurs and Mesdames
Wiseacres, to the battlefield and an addition
of generals on either side makes easy victory
for the other.   Take your equation to the
kitchen and apply it to the cooks and what becomes of your broth?   Apply it to medicine
and you will reason like the Indian who
thought that if two pills were good, a box
would be better.   He became at once one of
the so-called best Indians.   Of course, if
Wiseacre wishes to apply his equation to the
narrow field of mathematics, and believe me,
there is no narrower, and if he uses the word
" makes " in a sense in which it doesn't mean
" make," then he can take what pleasure he
pleases in the narrow, shrunken, two-penny
fragment of truth left to him.   But if Wiseacre will speak of the things that count, of
socialism and suffragettes, of cold-water and
home-rule, then his truism is a falsism.

We do not say Mr. Chesterton wrote that, but we are sure he could make the contradictory of any proposition more plausible than the writer of the above paragraph has succeeded in doing. Mr. Chesterton is clever; he is agile; he is infinitely amusing, but as Newman said of Cicero and his ingenuity, " he even hurts a good cause by excess of plausibility." Indeed cleverness may even go so far as to destroy the prime requisites of all style, truth and sincerity.

Here, then, is a brief and useful formula for cleverness: Be agile; abound in contrasts; reconcile contradictories; harmonize the remote and incongruous. If united with the requisite qualities of mind, this rule will perpetuate the supply of cleverness necessary to our dull existence.

XII
TABB AND FANCY

XII

TABB AND FANCY

FATHER TABB calls poetry

A silence, shell-like breathing from afar
The rapture of the deep.

Let us take up the shell that he offers us
and put it to our ear. It is not " the
wreathed horn " of a Triton, but smaller,
with delicate hues and fine lines, and before
we listen to its low murmur of the far-off
deep, we shall examine it. We shall consider
the medium made use of by the poet to convey his melodies to us. What is the language, and what the numbers in which he
expresses his suggestive thoughts, his breathings of the deep? What, in a word, is the
material and ornamentation of his poetic
shell? We are not surprised to find, having
ample evidence of Father Tabb's good taste
in the work before us, that he seeks for
no effect in the strangeness of vocabulary
or in the torturing of words to make them
disclose a meaning beyond them. Simple,

usual, intelligible words, neither eccentrically Anglo-Saxon nor heavily Latin, make up his vocabulary.

He has, then, fashioned his shell out of conventional material, nor has he been over-lavish in its ornamentation, subordinating sense to sound. The meter, however, has not been neglected, and his studies in it are evidenced by a clever imitation of Swinburne's " Anapests." Thus he sings of Magdalen:

Lo, the flame that hath driven her
Downward is quenched; and her grief like a flood
In the strength of a rain-swollen torrent hath
    shriven her:
Much hath she loved and much is forgiven her.

We must, indeed, have music in our verse, and its abundance in the poetic product of the day shows that the market is not yet overstocked with the luxury. Willingly, then, do we allow our ears to be tickled by

A flight of Fancy fitlier feigned for thee,

especially if such melodious tinkling be not too frequent, and the author be not allured by alliteration into any less happy feats of fancy, as one might consider, " the splendor of surprise spun by the sun around himself to behold the violet rise." Word-painting is

not pushed to extremes, and the Tennysonian style is not overdone; indeed it rarely occurs. "Blossom-bald," said of the dande-
lion when shorn of its flower and white seed-
ball, is Tennysonian in cloth and cut; and
such choice descriptions, as this of the humming bird,

> A flash of harmless lightning,
> A mist of rainbow dyes,
> The burnished sunbeams brightening,

will never pall. Indeed as we turn over in
our hands this fair shell in which Father
Tabb speaks to us, we find nothing there to
repel us, but much pleading on its pink lips
to lean our ear to it and listen to all the melodies it brings to us from its master.

In this fancy of the shell, which we have
been following with some want of clearness,
by comparing the shell itself to the words of
the poem and its murmur to their meaning,
in this fancy, I say, our author expresses to
us one of the great truths about good poetry.
Poetry is a whisper with a world of meaning.
Nay, it is silence itself, as he tells us, loud
with the roar of the ocean. It is a seed
which bears its harvest in the mind, a sesame
which opens to the more avaricious imagination richer treasures than fell beneath the eye

of Aladdin. Such is Homer's " ἐμὸν δ᾽
ἐγέλασσε φίλον κῆρ " (Od. ix., 413), and Shakespeare's " uncertain glory of an April day,"
and Tennyson's " Such a tide as moving
seems asleep."   Who, that is acquainted with
the time and place and person, fails to see the
world of meaning in Odysseus' laughter of
heart?   Then the threatening storm, the
passing shower, the breaking and swiftly
travelling clouds, the sudden unearthly
splendor after the rain, all this and more is
bound up within the narrow compass of " uncertain glory."   Finally who that has seen
the tide rising and sweeping in in long swells,
without roar, without foam, without churn-
ing waters or dashing waves, crowding
dumbly and persistently in among the piles
of the pier, who, having seen such a tide, does
not feel that its memory comes back to him
at the magic words, " moving seems asleep "?
Here is shell-like breathing of the deep.
These are examples of Holmes's meer-
schaum-pipe style of poetry, poetry with a
power to absorb and retain our best sympa-
thies, poetry capable of taking up into itself
any store of color that our imagination can
supply.

We look for examples of such poetry in
our author, and our search is rewarded with
success, though not signal or complete.   We

may cite the words of the author in his lines
on " Compensation ":

> How many a suppliant wave of sound
>   Must still unheeded roll,
> For one low utterance that found
>   An echo in my soul!

and say that there are some low utterances in
the poems before us which elicit a sympa-
thetic echo in the soul, among many which
pass by unheeded. As examples of such utterances, such shell-like breathings, we might
venture to offer the following:

> They lived and loved and died apart,
> But soul to soul and heart to heart.
>
> The evening cloud . . .
> Upborne upon a waveless heaven
>   Of radiant rest.

and of a swallow,

> Vanished thy form upon the wings of thought,
> Ere yet its place the lagging vision caught.

It will be noticed that these and the like
lines have, in general, their peculiar value,
independent of similitudes or imagery or even
poetic diction, but their wonderful force lies
in their suggestiveness. They are crystalli-
zations from long and intense experience;

they have caught and expressed the soul, the essence of things, and in expressing that, express all.

However, it is not such poetry which makes up the bulk of our author's productions. There is another good but inferior kind of poetry, whose beauty is felt and exhausted at the first reading, whose whole purpose is to set forth the resemblance which exists between two objects, and having accomplished that, spends its energy. We may go back to it, indeed, to admire the discernment and observation shown in detecting the resemblance, to praise the art and state of the composition, to be delighted with the nice skill that balances original and likeness, but in the meaning of the lines we look for nothing further. This poetry appeals to the head and not to the heart; it will take on no further coloring from our imagination; it will absorb no feeling; it is not the lasting daylight, ever revealing new beauties, but a flash that startles, delights and passes away. Of this poetry are such lines as these:

> Are ye ghosts of fallen leaves,
> O flakes of snow?

> 'Tis Christmas night! the snow,
> A flock unnumbered lies.

The shepherd stars from their fleecy cloud
Strode out on the night to see;
The Herod north-wind blustered loud.

In a word, this poetry is the product of fancy, as the former was of imagination, and this poetry of fancy forms the greater part of Father Tabb's poems.

Let not the reader, however, mistake our meaning, and think less of Father Tabb's work because of what we have said. The poetry of fancy is indeed poetry and good poetry, though it be not so noble or such a perennial fount of thought and feeling as the poetry of imagination. In saying, therefore, that our author's work is mostly fancy, it is only meant that he does not, in general, rise to the highest level of the best poetry. Short poems expressing one thought only, setting forth some analogy detected by a nice fancy, and carefully worked out in detail, characterize his verse. Let others raise the huge columns or bend over them great arches, this workman is content to beat away at capital or keystone, and if he carve there a flower, a leaf, perfect in every line, he is glad. His fancy has discerned a likeness which manifests itself only to the inward eye of the poet, and then he sets about his work. Down goes " as " to be shortly followed by " so," and then word is carefully added to word and fitted and polished until all be perfect.   Take for example the latter half of the beautiful sonnet, " Unuttered ":

So in my soul, a dream ineffable,
  Expectant of the sunshine or the shade,
Hath oft upon the brink of twilight chill,
  Or at the dawn's pale glimmering portal stayed
In tears, that all the quivering eyelids fill,
  In smiles that on the lip of silence fade.

Here you have " so " following after " as," and then begins the interplay and balancing of sunshine and shade, brink and portal, twilight and dawn, tears and smiles, lip and eye, fill and fade.   The same interplay will be found between the two parts of the sonnet.   The " as " and " so " are the scale pans, and the ear and mind of the poet are not satisfied until perfect balance results. This is the general character of Father Tabb's work, and it brings no small pleasure to the earnest and appreciative reader, when the author's fancy is at its best.   Of course, at times, the comparison is too minutely and too carefully worked out, and a feeling of artificiality is evident, which is the case in some of the longer verses; or again the fancy is less happy, and the reader, not with much

pleasure, we think, will chance on such lines
as

> Leafless, stemless, floating flower,

said of a butterfly, and

> What hand with spear of light
> Hath cleft the side of night,
> And from the red wound wide
> Fashioned the dawn, his bride?

We will not pause to notice the frequent
recurrence to the same ideas; for example,
on Photographs, Shadows and the Dew, until
even the fertile fancy of Father Tabb seems
exhausted.   We will not notice the fondness
shown for introducing ideas on the science of
Physics.   We must go on and strive to get a
truer estimate of our poet by contrasting him
with Herrick on the one hand and Wordsworth on the other.   Father Tabb is not, as
Herrick, simple, outspoken, fresh as nature,
wholly taken up with the object which has attracted the attention of his muse.   Herrick
forgets himself in his theme, as is well exemplified in his familiar lines on " Blossoms ";
but our poet always describes under the guid-
ance of head, not of heart, and never ventures
out of himself without looking back every
step to his fancy.   His muse is to his mind

and fancy what whisper, in his own poem, is
to silence:

> She ventures as a timorous child from land
> Still glancing at each wary step around,
> Lest suddenly she lose her sister's hand.

Nor in thus having recourse to fancy to interpret nature is he, like Wordsworth, seiz-
ing and portraying the nobler thoughts in-
spired by " the meanest flower that blows."
Witness Wordsworth's lines on " The
Daisy ":

> Do thou as thou art wont, repair
> My heart with gladness, and a share
> Of thy meek nature.

Our author occupies a middle ground.
Now he draws near to Herrick, as in his ana-
creontic lines on the " Brook " or in his beautiful " Fern Song," which we give:

> Dance to the beat of the rain, little Fern,
> And spread out your palms again,
> And say, " Tho' the sun
> Hath my vesture spun,
> He had labored, alas, in vain,
> But for the shade
> That the cloud hath made,
> And the gift of the Dew and the Rain?"
> Then laugh and upturn
> All your fronds, little fern,
> And rejoice in the beat of the rain!

Again he approaches to the sublimity of Wordsworth's interpretations of nature. It will be very interesting to compare Herrick's " Blossoms," Wordsworth's " Daisy " and the following little gem of the author called " Blossom ":

> For this the fruit, for this the seed,
>   For this the parent tree;
> The least to man, the most to God —
>   A fragrant mystery
> Where Love, with Beauty glorified,
>   Forgets Utility.

There is, too, among our author's devotional poems one that reminds us of Wordsworth in simplicity of language and depth and dignity of meaning. The poem is entitled, " The Assumption ! "

> Nor Bethlehem nor Nazareth
>   Apart from Mary's care;
> Nor heaven itself a home for Him
>   Were not His mother there.

Good, true devotional poetry is quite another thing from pious exclamations in meter and rime, and to write poetry which really inspires devotion, which has the burning eloquence of a noble sermon, is a difficult task. Despite its difficulty, it has found in Father Tabb a writer fully able to cope with it. His poetry on sacred subjects is really excellent. It abounds, it is true, in fancy, as his other poems and is, so far, wanting in that reverent simplicity, directness, and fulness of meaning which mark the best of Herrick's " Noble Numbers "; as, for example, one of his Christmas Carols from which we take these beautiful lines:

> We see Him come, and know Him ours,
> Who, with His sunshine, and His showers
> *Turns all the patient ground to flowers.*

Nevertheless, though Father Tabb may not equal Herrick in the qualities we have mentioned, his verses on religious subjects have the true ring of poetry about them and a more Catholic tone and are always fit to read and they will not fail to find their way into our hearts, leaving us the better for it. Indeed, in every line there is cheering and elevating sentiment, no clouds of despair nor piteous moanings, no languishing, maudlin love lyrics done up in curiously wrought French meters and rimes, no hazy wilderness of words where the sense stumbles and loses itself in shadows, perfumes, sounds and colors. May some one be able to write of him in times to come, as he has written of Keats in what we consider, after " Unmoored," his most beautiful sonnet:

> Thus, on the scroll of Nature, everywhere,
> Thy name, a deathless syllable, remains.

XIII
POETRY AND INTEREST

XIII

POETRY AND INTEREST

THE members of the theatrical company are peering through convenient holes in the scenery with heart-chills at the empty seats and heart-thrills where they see unbroken ranks of the audience. Only the leading man or the old-timer holds off in disdain or affected indifference, but give them a clear stage, and the glued eye steals a surreptitious glance. The arts want an audience. The poet may appear more indifferent than speaker or actor because the audience is not so immediate or pressing a need, but no poet will be content to soliloquize or issue closet poems for a select clientele. A poet does not wish to be a mere carver of bric-a-brac. He has a message, and he does not sing it to the empty air. If his audience is not now filling up the seats in front of his stage, he hopes that from years and centuries and cycles, he may gradually call enough listeners of his message to gratify at least his prophetic eye.

The poet mourns for his lost inheritance,

when he was the bard who issued religious
oracles, the minstrel who embodied his country's heroes in stirring verse, or the trouba-
dour who sang of love and home and war.
He is ill-content with the bottom of the maga-
zine page when his ancestors were in temple
and castle.   Not the orator only, but the
poet and all artists strive each in his own way
to be popular, and the poet ought to feel the
pulse of the people, if he would avoid the
hieroglyphics of mere symbolism by thinking
to himself, or become maudlin and incoherent
by talking to himself.

Homer talked to his fellow-men and kept
his feet on earth and his head out of the
clouds.   He took the story-songs which the
people liked, and in them he delivered his
message.   The epic after Homer grew conventional and artificial and retired into a
closet.   Then poetry went out again where
the people were and took their songs, which,
in course of time, etherealized into subtle
lyrics and drifted into the closet.   Once more
the people were approached and their village
masks and rude miracle plays were lifted by
art into the drama.   Will the drama of to-
day succumb to the popular picture plays?
Will it stereotype into a fossil and remain in
a closet, or will it, as seems more likely, be
rejuvenated by touch with the " movies " and

display new forms of art. Pastoral poetry followed a like course, from the people to Theocritus, to Virgil, to Italian and French poetical shepherds and shepherdesses, who most likely could not tell a sheep from a goat.

Poetry, then, is not content with the closet; it insists on being abroad and in touch with the people. If its various species become conventional they are discarded for what the people like; if its forms lose their spontaneity by hardening into rigid moulds, the moulds are broken, and fresh forms are sought; if the language is transformed into fossil ornamentation, a Wordsworth will wish to have poetry frankly speak in the language of the people. Browning will rebel against the smoothness of line and ease of rime; Patmore will chafe at the shackles of verse which Whitman will utterly break; Kipling, following Thespis and Tyrtaeus and Theocritus, fares forth to life and comes back with new quarrying from the rough cliffs, ready for poetry's enhancing sculpture and polish. Then, again, art and conventionality and decay.

Poetry will be heard, and why should it not? The poet claims to be a seer, and have visions of the truth not vouchsafed to other men. He is on fire with his message. He will not be a mere revealer of nature and lux-

uriate in the asphodel meadows of sheer description, whose abundance too often means
mental barrenness for the readers. He
might poetize a star, as a painter paints it,
"when only one is shining in the sky," content simply to reveal its beauty in its perfect
being, its ontological truth and ontological
beauty, we might term it. That will be a
poem indeed, but he will see other truths in a
star, truths of knowledge, intellectual truths,
and he will manifest their perfection and
beauty. Beauty is the handmaid of truth;
the luster and resplendence of reality. The
poet will reveal the truth of judgments or
logical truth, and his audience will again taste
the fine flavor of the beauty found in logical
truth and will experience the delights of mental appreciation which are the proper and
peculiar harvest of beauty. The poet is not
yet content. There is more truth still in his
star. "The heavens are telling the glory of
God" and the poet will with the Psalmist see
the law of God in the firmament on high.
The poet will have visions of moral truth
and will want his listeners to act in accord-
ance with them. He will have recourse to
the grandeur of eloquence. Then the good,
which is the source of emotion and of all action, will be vested by poetry with appropriate beauty. The poet will reveal the beauty

of joy, the beauty of desire, of hope, of love, of good, and thus he will reach with the help of eloquence to the heart of the people.

So have acted all the poets. Professor Murray would have us believe that the legion whose name according to him is Homer, expurgated Greek religion of many of its cruelties to teach a higher morality. David taught in his psalms and Isaiah in his prophecies and Job in his lamentations as well as Horace with aurea mediocritas. Wearing the mask of apparent beauty and apparent good, come the evil teachers, Shelley with his revolt and atheism and Swinburne with his hedonism. The poets will have an audience; they will teach, not like professors, but rather like prophets. They lay open their truths to our intuition rather than to our reasoning powers. They do not drag us through a syllogism, but entrance us with a vision wherein truth and beauty are united. Eloquence will reach out its hand to poetry when eloquence is aflame with love of good. Then poetry will fascinate the mind with its high beauty and eloquence will capture the heart with its entrancing good, and like a chivalrous and fiery knight with his fair lady, they will attract the eyes of the world. Poetry will have its audience.

XIV
NOVELTY OR ECCENTRICITY

XIV

NOVELTY OR ECCENTRICITY

NEWSPAPERS have been exploiting in recent years the novelty or, if you will, eccentricities of modern art. Futurists and Cubists and their kind have bewildered us with their vagaries, and humorists and caricaturists have revelled in the new field opened to them. It is sadly to be feared that some of these strange productions owe their origin to the modern desire for exclusive attention. That one should be noticed is an appetite created or, at least, highly stimulated by press and advertising, and it is not at all surprising that some lack of discrimination should be shown in choosing the adequate means to attract notice. On the other hand, however, a great deal of extravagance in literature and art is due to sincere, if mistaken, ideas concerning the nature and medium of art. No one can fail to sympathize with the ambition of those who would galvanize fossil conventionalities with new life, but every one must earnestly desire that these misguided energies be diverted into proper channels. What, then, is the right way to work for novelty in literature and art?

Language, like men in Shelley's poem, looks before and after. It looks on to the listener or reader and back to the speaker or writer. It should not attract attention to itself, but, as a perfect mirror or a transparent windowpane, it should be lost to sight while transmitting or reflecting the author's thought to the mind he addresses. In a good writer we have to make an effort to center attention upon his words and style, and when the style is such as to call attention to itself and distract from the subject under discussion, there is a defect or at least something lacking in the perfection of style. There is a flaw in the mirror. The window may be handsome, may be the finest stained-glass, but it does not fulfill the prime purpose of a window; it is not a transparent medium. When an author strives to be interesting, he may be tempted to display stained-glass windows; he may lay undue stress on the medium instead of keeping his eyes fixed on the thought he wishes to convey and the mind to which it is to be conveyed. Now in language, which is the medium of the art of literature, there are two things that may be made prominent and interfere with the trans-

mission of thought; these are the sound and
the sense.   Any juggling with sound or sense,
any undue attempt to make language a thing
of beauty in itself and apart from its message
will in the end defeat the very purpose of
language. The results may please, may
rivet attention, but they will have a wrong
direction. We shall be attracted to the
search-light itself, not to the object on which
it levels its beams.
What is true of language and the art of
literature is true of all mediums of all arts.
The true musician is forgotten; he is hidden
in a sea of sound, as Shelley's poet is "hidden
in the light of thought." We do not think
of him; we are borne away on the waves of
his melody. But let him announce that he
will perform a sonata of Beethoven on one
string, or let him mimic cathedral chimes and,
to make the imitation more realistic, let him,
as we have seen it done, sway his violin to
copy the movements of a bell's tongue, then
all attention is fixed upon the musician. The
medium becomes more important than the
melody; dexterity usurps the place of art. A
painter will win your notice to his portrait
or scene, not to the colors and outlines. If
you wish to see these, you will have to force
yourself by reflection to do so. Suppose,
however, that your painter, instead of draw-

ing a head of Christ in the way Da Vinci or
Murillo or Hoffmann would draw it, should
produce a face of the Savior drawn by one
continuous stroke of the pencil, as has been
done by a clever draughtsman — in that case
you would not be able to see the portrait for
the lines.   You would admire the skill of
hand, the triumph of ingenuity; you would
applaud the successful overcoming of difficulties, but you would be giving your praise not
to a work of art but to a " tour de force."

The same principle of undue straining of
the medium of art is exemplified in sculpture.
Language will degenerate from its perfection
as a medium of art if it is unduly stressed
either on its material or on its formal side, if
its sounds are overemphasized or the sense is
distracting.   So sculpture may degenerate.
All art may be looked upon as a translation;
it is the expression in its proper medium of
the thoughts and emotions of the artist.   In
the medium of art, as in language, there is a
material and formal element.   As, therefore, we forget the catgut or wire in music,
the vibrating vocal chords in a speech and the
oil and pigments in a painting, so we should
forget the marble in a statue.   Will some of
our modern sculptors let us do so?   We
speak as amateurs, who look on sculpture to
understand it and enjoy it, and we must an-

swer that we cannot get at the statuary because the marble is obtruding itself, either by letting us on the one hand never forget it is marble, or on the other by endeavoring to make marble express what it cannot possibly do. There is an undue stress put upon both the material and formal elements of the medium. Take Rodin's "Hand of God." You have a rough fragment of marble and a forearm with a hand protruding from the marble. You cannot get away from the medium. You are forcibly detained there. The artist has tried to make marble mean what it cannot mean. He has carved out a symbol, not a statue, and when you have seen the answer to the puzzle, you turn away marvelling at the dexterity, not entranced by the art. The man who would break off that solitary forearm and hand, and scoop out the dolls from the palm and suspend the fragment in the archeological section of a museum will do service to art. Then the visitors will see a hand splendidly carved, not, as it is now, a bewildering dream. Rodin has been fanciful. When translating his thoughts into stone, he forgot the limitations of his medium, forgot that he must make his marble a representation of something intelligible to the spectator and not a hieroglyphic.

No one has bettered Aristotle's profound concept that art is a re-presentation, an imitation, a staging of nature. The very pleasure of art is found in the surprise that, by paint and stone and sound and gesture, nature is enacted on a new and separate stage, devoid of nature's imperfections. Yet the artist may not forget how much he is conditioned by his medium. Else he will have the midsummer madness of "A Midsummer Night's Dream," where men play the parts of plaster and of moon and of chinks in the wall. One thing above all else which might make him so forget is the ambition and desire for originality. The master painters and sculptors have embodied noble thoughts in noble forms. Their modern successors, not blessed with nobler ideals which might afford a better field for competition with the masters, seek for originality in the medium. With paint and stone and sound they outrival Bottom's versatile actors in the rôles which they would force the medium of every art to sustain. Music is making frantic efforts for recognition by variously dislocated discords. The American Indian, the African Negro, the Chinese, the Tartars and others have been made to disgorge their earliest freaks of music, which correspond to the mud-pie stage of sculpture. Then again various and most elaborate imitative effects have been embodied in sounds, or at least printed on the program. The farm, the shipwreck, the boiler factory, have been enacted in sound. To-morrow we may have the Subway Glide and the Bridge Crush, with screams and oaths and pushing and trampling on toes and grinding of wheels and clanging bells and intermittent suicides.

Perhaps musical sounds have already, forgetful of their limitations, played the moon with Bottom's fellows. But sounds have been outdistanced by lines and pigments in the wild chase for originality. Impressionists, Post-Impressionists, Cubists, Futurists, have been torturing their medium into various puzzles. They want to derive from paint what cannot possibly be expressed by it; they are not content to strain their medium; they fracture it. If these attempts continue, we may find sculpture discarding marble and bronze and substituting wine-jelly in order to get a realistic reproduction of life and its ceaseless agitation, or we may find a Futurist mounting a canvas of scrambled paint on a milk-shaker or on an automobile to produce the impression of vibration and speed. There would be no mistaking the realism; there would surely be novelty; you will undoubtedly see the paint, but what of the picture?

Novelty in art is desirable, not for itself or at any price, but only in strict subordination to the artist's ideals.   Interest in literature, often the outcome of novelty, is not to be won by the undue emphasis of expression. The speaker in search of interest must not concentrate his energies on words but on the thought.   Distraction is not interest, and the energy that is taken up in wondering at the expression is dissipated by misdirection. The writer or speaker must indeed put his thoughts in a new way, if he would interest. But he must have novelty without distraction, and he must not abuse his medium on its material or on its formal side.   Let him put a new glass in the old frames or burnish up the panes, that the light of his thought may stream through clearly and freshly, but let him not be novel at the expense of the thought, filling his language with colors and forms which delight but distract.   In his language colors are not an end in themselves, as they are in a cathedral window, which, unlike ordinary windows, is not to be looked through; its purpose is to give a dim, religious light, and edify while it softly illuminates.   A writer eschews stained-glass.

What are some of the ways in which language is obtrusive and distracting?   It may
be, like music, too imitative.   Language, it
is true, does suggest by its letters and syl-
lables various sounds and may by a word or
two almost reproduce a sound, but, if it
strives to do more, it goes beyond its proper
sphere.   Marble and paint are not moving
things and, even when transformed to art,
are motionless.   They can suggest activity.
If they are ultra-realistic and strive to reproduce it, they attract attention to themselves.   If a painter should construct an
actual waterfall of flowing paint or a sculptor put a marble horse on rockers, the spectators could not restrain their laughter any
more than they could when looking at
Horace's conglomerate.   Poetry may go
farther than prose in imitative effects, yet
excess is possible, there, too.   Poe's " Bells "
represents   perhaps   the   extreme   limit.
Southey's " How the Water Came Down at
Lodore " is a mere " tour de force," an ab-
breviated rhyming dictionary.   You cannot
see the water for the words.   In prose one
recalls with pleasure Newman's famous passage in the " Present Position of Catholics,"
describing the charges of the Anglican bishops during the disturbances connected with
the so-called Papal Aggression.   The like-

ness which Newman draws between the expressions of the bishops and the peals of the bells is helped out by the ding-dong of the reiterated and reechoing adjectives There too the slight exaggeration gives added zest to the humor of the description. Only a great artist can handle such devices gracefully. An inferior writer would have overdone it.

Not often, however, is the writer or speaker tempted to err by unduly emphasizing the material elements of his language, either in the imitative way just mentioned or in any other traits of style connected with the sounds of words, such as alliteration, noticeable rhythm, metrical scansion in prose, elaborate balancing. All these are good things when used in proper moderation; all defective when they are used simply for their own sake and attract attention to themselves. It is rather in the formal elements of their medium that the speaker and writer are more tempted to exceed. They may stretch a likeness too far, making what would be excellent as a simple metaphor strained and distracting in a forced allegory. They may go far afield for a comparison which, because it is an exotic, succeeds better in fixing attention upon itself than upon what it was intended to illustrate. As fatal a

fault in literature as it would be for a show-
man to use his most stupendous freak as a
barker. No one would go into the show.
They would stay outside and look at the
barker.

The titles of old controversial works will
furnish many amusing examples of stretching a comparison beyond all bounds. One
controversialist would write a book and put
on the title-page: "The weasel of truth
which tracks the rodent of error to its most
secret lairs, dislodges him from his hole and
dispatches with the sharp tooth of effective
argument." Then his adversary would respond with a ponderous tome, entitled:
"The pebbles of David, picked from the
field of fact, discharged with the right arm
of bold indignation, delivered upon the
brazen forehead of giant impudence and lay-
ing low a veritable Goliath of monstrous im-
piety." However, not all extension of metaphors is defective. It is possible to carry
a resemblance through a paragraph, or even
several paragraphs, if due caution is exercised. The author has his eye constantly
fixed on the two objects compared, and,
wherever the resemblance is suitable, he expresses it suggestively, not boldly, and so
contrives to reveal the truth clearly without
distracting the attention to the language.

Newman is a master in this art.   Sometimes his metaphor, like the bony frame in the body, will extend throughout a paragraph, and give unity and shape to the thought by making the comparison felt rather than by baring its presence.   In one paragraph of the "Second Spring," near the end, Newman expresses a comparison of warfare in at least a dozen different terms, and all is done so skilfully that deliberate and careful reflection is required to detect the fact.   In the spoken word it would have been even less evident, but the picture would still have been felt and would have enkindled the emotions of those who heard.

These few instances will suffice to show how the literary artist may get novelty without unduly accentuating his medium, either in sound or in sense.   Examples of successful and unsuccessful novelty in literature might be multiplied.   In fact, we believe that most of the instances of what is called fanciful and fantastic in prose and poetry may be ascribed to this very attempt on the part of the writer to force his medium into prominence, by undue emphasis either on its formal or on its material side.   This explanation of fancy, now a somewhat disused term of art criticism, will, we believe, account for most, if not all, the accepted meanings of that elusive term. However that may be, this at least is certain: many of the fads and vagaries in all modern arts are the outcome of desperate attempts at originality by straining the artistic medium. Newness, freshness and originality in art and literature come from within; they are the fruits of thought and earnest idealization; they subdue the artistic medium and make it lose itself in expression.

XV
NEED OF IMAGINATION

THE NEED OF IMAGINATION

TO interest is one thing; to amuse is quite another thing. Amusement is diverting; interest is concentrating. Interest looks forward to something beyond, but amusement, though, like everything else, it may at times be directed to a further purpose, finds usually a center in itself and rests there. Interest, however, looks beyond and is intended to capture the attention of the mind and center it upon something. We are interested *in* things; we are amused *with* things. In the chapters of this book we have been discussing interest as brought about by language and by thought through language.

Interest may indeed be awakened by the subject itself about which a man speaks or writes or even by something outside of the speech or article. In Webster's famous definition of eloquence, he imagines an occasion of supreme importance, a crisis, where language is hardly needed. With the enemy at the

door there is no need of striving by language
to awaken interest. The enemy does that.
In university lectures for the students who
are earnest in their specialty, the teacher
needs no help from word or style to interest
his listeners and readers. The subject does
that. But there are subjects to which people are indifferent and should be aroused;
there are important occasions, and their importance is not recognized through the blind-
ness or indifference of men; there are times
when even enthusiasts are wearied or slum-
bering. The language must interest then,
must awaken and hold attention. Words
are its only instrument; these are the wealth
by which language attracts, the weapons by
which it conquers, the pleasure with which
it allures and sates those to whom it appeals.

Language has the function of teaching, of
conveying truth, and for that language must
be clear; it has the function of proposing motives for action to the will and for that language must stir up love or hate through good
or evil as moving forces, and for that end
language is said to be forceful. But there
remains another function of language, not
indeed as important or as necessary as the
function of conveying truth or proposing motives, but decidedly useful and, in the case of
the distracted, tired and fickle mental pow-

ers of man, quite necessary as a condition, if not as a cause, of effectiveness in writing and speaking.

What is the name of that quality of style? The ancients called it pleasure or charm; moderns call it ease, vivacity, beauty and elegance. I have chosen the term, interest, because though the other terms for the most part express the idea and in some cases with more exclusive definiteness, yet interest shows more the practical nature of this function of style and serves to keep distinctly before the speaker or writer the mind for which the truth must be made attractive. It is good for an author to feel that he must interest.

With the exception of epigrams and certain figures which affect the words alone, the chief source of that interest has been shown to be in the imagination. The necessity of the imagination is often asserted by writers on style. The Abbé Mullois in his excellent work, *The Clergy and the Pulpit*, says: "You must first attract the people by the senses, the imagination, by sentiment and by the heart. The people like to be interested and moved. After a week spent in absorbing material drudgery, their poor souls require the breath of the divine word to animate and cheer them. To them espe-

cially religion should be glad tidings. We
should set out by making them feel and bless,
but instead of that we begin with reasoning
and end with the same. We have a rage for
reasoning. . . . We must insist therefore
on the necessity of giving the people a right
direction; not the dry, cold direction of a
metaphysical argument or of a sword's
point, but a benevolent impulse." Potter in
his *Art of Extempore Speaking* declares:
" It is easy enough, or at all events it is not
very difficult, to speak of things in general,
to treat an abstract subject in a vague and
abstract way."

Besides testimony, the history of language, the teaching of philosophy, the evidence of experience, go to show that the
mind works with and through the imagination, which is the store-house of sense per-
ceptions. The spiritual, the immaterial,
can be understood only through analogy and
comparison with the material. The imagination of the author, as a material faculty,
has stored away in it the analogies necessary
to make the abstract and immaterial concrete and tangible to the imagination of the
reader.

Examine an interesting writer; study the
sources of interest in any speaker and you
will find them dwelling on what is particular,

not indefinite, on what is specific and concrete, not generic and abstract, on what is
local, what is individual, actual and personal
in its appeal. "It is detail alone," says
Lacordaire, "that speaks to the eyes and to
the heart." "The thoughts which serve as
starting points should always be simple, natural and popular. The people do not understand abstractions or speculations of reason, which are to them a strange language.
You should start from the known and lead
them to the unknown. You must begin
with sensible, visible, actual things in order
to draw them gently toward spiritual and
invisible things." (Mullois.) All these
sources of interest are derived from the material faculty of the imagination, whereas
the abstract, general, universal are the work
of the mind.

Translate for example a well known passage from the concrete into the abstract.
The passage is not as technical or metaphysical as it might easily be made without exaggeration. It runs as follows: "Divine
Providence has given excellences to the
world such as the wealthiest of men did not
possess, and the Providence which did that,
will care for you." This statement is clear;
but how tame, cold, lifeless and colorless
compared with the divine original, so famil-

iar and yet after many repetitions still vivid and effective! " Consider the lilies of the field, how they grow. They labor not, neither do they spin; and yet I say to you that not even Solomon in all his glory was arrayed as one of these. Now if God so clothe the grass of the field which to-day is and to-morrow is not, how much more you, O yet of little faith."

Does the strict argumentation of this passage lose any of the force because it is clothed in concrete terms? Nothing is indefinite or abstract; everything particular, local, actual and personal.

Consider again the statement in the *Summa* (III, 6, 6): " The cause of Christ's interior sorrow was all the sins of the human race for which He was satisfying by His suffering. Hence He ascribes them, as it were, to Himself, saying with the psalmist, ' the words of my sins.' " Contrast now Newman's wonderful amplification of that proposition in his sermon on the *Mental Sufferings of Our Lord in His Passion:* " There He knelt, motionless and still, while the horrible and vile fiend clad his spirit in a robe steeped in all that is hateful and heinous in human crime, which clung close around His Heart and filled His conscience and found its way into every sense

and pore of His mind, and spread over Him
a moral leprosy, till He almost felt Himself
that which He could never be, and which
His foe would fain have made Him. . . .
Are these the hands of the immaculate Lamb
of God, once innocent, but now red with
ten thousand barbarous deeds of blood?
Are these His lips, not uttering prayer and
praise and holy blessings, but defiled with
oaths and blasphemies and doctrines of
devils? . . . Hopes blighted, vows broken,
lights quenched, warnings scorned, opportu-
nities lost; the innocent betrayed, the young
hardened, the penitent relapsing, the just
overcome, the aged failing,"— and so on
through many details with the characteristic
exuberance of Newman's sermon style.

Facts, historical instances, narrations of
personal experience, dramatic dialog, these
come within the sphere of the imagination
and also render language interesting. "Another way of simplifying truth," says Mullois, "is by narrative, of which people are
very fond. They cast everything, even spiritual things, into tales, legends and facts.
We should imitate them by putting a moral
or dogmatic truth into action, connecting it
with a fact. Give it the form of a little
drama, making the truth to come and go, to
speak, question and reply." "Let the

speaker," declares Potter, " not be sparing in the use of narrations, since a judicious employment of histories, parables and examples is one of the most powerful ways of interesting an audience and retaining their attention."   Cicero in his speech for Archias has at least eight stories, which were no doubt developed and dramatized in the delivery, though they are condensed and made allusive in the published version.

XVI

DEVELOPING THE IMAGINATION

XVI

DEVELOPING THE IMAGINATION

TO write in an imaginative way is not by
any means easy. Reading and experience must have stored the imagination with
treasures, and reflection must bring these
treasures to the surface of the imagination in
the hour of composition. Modern researches
into the realms of the subconscious reveal
the fact, which our dreams amply corrobo-
rate, that the impressions of the senses will
remain for many years in the imagination.
Who knows whether any sight or sound
which has been perceived by a vigorous eye
and ear, is ever lost? It is startling to think
that all our past experience may be still with
us. If so, how can that imagination be
made to stand and deliver? Constant and
earnest reflection upon the writer's subject
will serve to stir the sluggish waters of the
past and make them disgorge their sunken
treasures. "The man who would amplify
with effect," says Potter, "must return
again to the very viscera of his argument for

the happy thoughts and the felicitous illustrations with which to develop it." Reflection awakens the associated images, and from their abundance one may choose abundantly. "An abstract and metaphysical treatment of a question," says Longhaye, "may be had with but half knowledge, but the striking concrete, popular statement of the truth is the fruit of perfect knowledge." The man of one truth is something of a bore, but everything is grist for his mill in the way he finds exemplifications of his truth and illustrative comparisons for his one truth on all sides.

Even old and trite metaphors which have lost their color may be brought back to fresh brilliance by reflection upon the comparison and by entering into the heart of the metaphor. "Our Holy Mother the Church" has become for most of us a mere idle word, but let the worn out thought be reminted in a glowing imagination and it will have all the brightness and ring of a first coinage. Note how the motherhood of the Church thrills with life in Newman's well known sermon on *The Parting of Friends*. "O Mother of Saints! O school of the wise! O nurse of the heroic! Of whom went forth, in whom have dwelt, memorable names of old, to spread the truth abroad, or

to cherish or illustrate it at home. . . . O
my mother, whence is this unto thee, that
thou hast good things poured out upon thee
and canst not keep them, and bearest children, yet darest not own them?"

Reflection will lead the way to realization.
Much writing is merely from verbal memory. Words have been heard or seen in
print; they remain in the verbal memory and
are used again without even being brought
into touch with the imagination, much less
with the personality of the writer. When
the writer heard or read his words, did he
realize them or did he see the reality which
they represented? When he learned a
word, did his imagination furnish a picture
of the thing? Or did the word find a place
in his memory only without touching his
imagination? Perhaps, the word, which
like all words was originally concrete in
meaning and pictured its object, had by the
time he came to know it lost its picturing
power and had become a mere symbol.
Such is the usual history of words. The
names we all have were once picturesque;
now they are mere signs or tags which distinguish us as numbers would. It is the
work of realization always to see the thing
through the word. That is a fruitful exercise of the imagination, developing the fac-

ulty by seeing the original picture of the word or of the reality the word represents. In translating from another language or in explaining the meaning to himself, the one who would be an imaginative writer will not have recourse to another word found in the memory, but will insist that his imagination furnish to him an instance, specific and definite, of the reality.

Another practice which will exercise the writer's imagination and vivify his style is to visualize his audience. The presence of the audience will serve as a tonic and while it suggests difficulties, it will spur on the writer to overcome the difficulties and bring· his message home. " A man," says Potter, " loses sight of his special audience, with its special needs and its special circumstances; he has no one, in particular in view in what he says, any more than he has any plain, precise and definite object clearly before him; he speaks of vague generalities in a vague general way which would apply to any audience equally as well as to the one he addresses. . . . It is easy to compose an instruction in the abstract and this is just what most men do. They deliver vague, general and impractical discourses . . . but what is needed is, not instruction in the abstract, but instruction in the concrete; in other words,

instruction, every word of which shall have
special and positive reference and application to the very people to whom it is addressed."

After reflection and realization comes
reading. Imaginative language, like any
other language, must be learned from those
who use it. Of all language that of poetry
is the most imaginative. That may be the
reason why so many writers of prose have
read and written poetry. Few have succeeded in both prose and verse, but who can
doubt that the prose of great writers from
Cicero to Newman was helped by poetry?
On the authority of Father "Mat" Russell
we have it that Father "Tom" Burke, the
great Dominican preacher, "read poetry
every day in order to gain as much vividness
and sweetness as he could for his language in
the pulpit." This is Father Burke's own
testimony. In the fields of science where we
should not expect it, we have a like testimony
from Tyndall. (*Life of Tennyson*, II,
470) "I do not know whether scientific men
generally have found the warming up of the
imagination as beneficial to them as it has
been to me." And quotes from his journal:
"I must now turn from Tennyson to whom
I had appealed for inspiration to Lefebre de
Fourcy, a dry mathematician." When called

poetical, he replied: "Be it so. If poetry make me a dreamer, so much the worse for me. If it make me work, so much the better."

That the imagination is affected by fiction cannot be denied. Yet though fiction excite the imagination, it will not be found to be the best means of developing the faculty. In poetry, we shall find the apt means for strengthening the imagination along the lines of its greatest usefulness. Fiction narrates in detail; poetry relies on suggestion. Fiction is diffuse; poetry· is forced by the requirements of meter and custom to be concentrated. In fiction, we listen passively to what another has imagined; the aim of good poetry is to stimulate the imagination of the reader and make him realize, without explicit statement, the crystallization of a poet's best experience. So much for methods; the superiority of subject matter in poetry needs no remark. The noblest thoughts and noblest emotions of the best minds are, and necessarily must be, the substance of the finest poetry. The range of fiction is unlimited, and its trend is earthward. Yet the prose writer must remember that his images and his language will be different from the language and images of poetry.

Choose, then, a good poem — a noble, elevated poem — characterized by lofty feeling, without a taint or suspicion of anything low, or mean, or debasing — a poem in which the quality of imagination is prominent. Then read and reread. " Now, I tell you," the *Autocrat of the Breakfast-Table* says, " a poem must be kept and used. A genuine poem is capable of absorbing an indefinite amount of the essence of our own humanity — its tenderness, its heroism, its regrets, its aspirations, so as to be gradually stained through with a divine color. It must take time to bring the sentiment of a poem in harmony with our nature by staining ourselves through every thought and image our being can penetrate." A perfect understanding is the supreme requisite. One cannot soar, if held down by the meaning. One cannot sound the depths, if kept on the surface. Read, therefore —

> Till the dilating soul, enrapt, transfused,
> Into the mighty vision passing — there
> As in her natural form, swell vast to heaven.

Take such a passage as Wordsworth's lines on the bust of Sir Isaac Newton:

> The marble index of a mind forever
> Voyaging on strange seas of thought, alone.

You may follow out the comparison suggested by "index," but, as this is fancy, no farther progress may perhaps be made than to admire the aptness of the comparison. The next line, however, opens up an extensive view. Let the imagination range over those seas; let it behold them in all the varied changes of storm and calm; let it fathom their depths and sweep their horizon, and peer farther and farther into their encircling haze to north, to south, to east, to west, and it will be ever in the wake of the lone wayfarer who was "the first that ever burst into that silent sea." Other lines of thought may be found, other scenes disclosed, or we may find other passages more suitable, but whatever the passage may be, if it is pure and noble, give the imagination free rein and its development will go on apace.

Nor is it to be feared that we are cultivating insincerity because we are, perhaps, discovering meanings the author never dreamt of. There are some golden words of Lowell which it would be well to remember in this connection: "He reads most wisely who thinks everything into a book that it is capable of holding; and it is the stamp and token of a great book so to incorporate itself with our own being, so to quicken our insight and stimulate our thought as to make us feel as if we helped to create it while we read.   Whatever we can find in a book that aids us in the conduct of life, or to a truer interpretation of it, or to a franker reconcilement with it, we may with a good conscience believe it is not there by accident, but the author meant we should find it there."   Even if the author had not the extent and fullness of meaning definitely before him, he is showing us something of nature, and the divine Artisan of Nature has left in His handiwork the traces of His infinite perfections which the mind of man may forever dwell upon and never exhaust.

XVII

IS ESTHETIC EMOTION A SPINAL THRILL?

XVII

IS ESTHETIC EMOTION A SPINAL THRILL?

ABOUT the beginning of last century the terms fancy and imagination entered largely into all literary criticism, and for much the greater part of the nineteenth century writers were busy defining, illustrating and applying the ideas of fancy and imagination to literature and art. Wordsworth in his *Prefaces*, Coleridge in his *Biographia Literaria*, were the pioneers. Leigh Hunt followed with his book, *Imagination and Fancy*. Ruskin in his *Modern Painters* developed the ideas, analyzed the imagination and fancy into species and applied the terms to painting. He afterwards spoke slightingly of this part of his work. Other critics, like Poe and Hutton, made use of the same terms. Philosophers followed in the wake of the critics and investigated the nature of fancy and imagination. But in more recent years there is less heard of these terms. What is the reason for this silence? It may be because readers have been surfeited with fancy and imagination, or that they did not understand very well what the terms meant, or could not follow the multiple varieties which each new critic added, or that they could not make out whether fancy and imagination were qualities in word or speech or faculties of the mind and, if the latter, whether they were distinct from each other and each divided into many species or simply two phases of the same faculty, and finally whether that faculty was the immaterial mind or some material power.

The trouble all along with these terms has been their vagueness. Those who used them had no consistent philosophy or definite theory of thought and could not speak of imagination and fancy without confusion. Coleridge brought in very early some of the terms of German idealistic philosophy and further complicated things by tangling up the imagination with personality and consciousness. He calls too the imagination an " esemplastic " faculty, but one diligent reader can find no tangible meaning in that learned phrase unless it signifies the mind applying an adjective to a noun or asserting a quality of a subject; in a word, the intellectual process of attribution, " a good man," and of predication,

"the man is good." Wordsworth and
Hunt kept away from the philosophy of the
subject, and by their illustrations led their
readers to identify imagination and fancy
not with any particular faculties. They
kept strictly to the products of these faculties in language. Ruskin rejects the explanation of a Scotch metaphysician and refers everything to mystery. Poe has a clear,
well-reasoned theory, easy at any rate to
understand, if it does not explain the whole
truth. He claims that imagination, fancy
and humor are all products of one and the
same faculty, the mind, which by attribution
or predication brings two or more ideas together. When the combination satisfies us
as being true and natural, we have imagination; if the combination startles by its novelty, we have fancy; if the combined elements are incongruous, we have humor.

More recent literary criticism has made
a fetich of emotion. Imagination had some
meaning, but what meaning is attached to
emotion by many critics it is very hard to
determine. Imagination too was nearer to
the truth because imagination is a faculty of
knowing, and beauty, the object of literature, effects subjectively a pleasure of the
cognitive faculty. Besides, the term, imagination, is not exposed to the excesses of the

term, emotion.   If imagination was a cloak
for ignorance, what shall we say of emotion?
A professor of theology used to warn his
class that it was a good thing to know the
precise point where reason ended and where
mystery began.   It was not good theology
to cry mystery when the mind grew weary or
was deficient in acumen.   Neither is it good
criticism to cry emotion when nobody knows
just what is meant by emotion.

In a splendid book, the *Principles of Literary Criticism,* which is sane and sound despite its philosophy or lack of philosophy,
Professor Winchester, the author, on every
page speaks of literature in terms of emotion, and yet refuses to define emotion.   " I
have not thought it necessary," he states,
" to enter into any investigation of the nature and genesis of emotion " (p. 55).   If
the author wishes to make emotion the essential element in literature, he need not of
course be able to comprehend fully what
emotion is and how it is generated, but he
should have at least a definite objective
meaning to the term, which would identify
it for the mind when he uses the term.

Such a definite meaning would have saved
him from inconsistency in saying that " emotions are motives, as their name implies;
they induce the will; they decide the whole

current of life " (p. 48), and then later (p. 63) rejecting from literature all self-regarding emotions. All action, it is well known, originates in good, and every emotion appealing to the will is self-regarding. Again a definite meaning for emotion would have kept him from making one difference between imagination and fancy to be that imagination awakens emotion and fancy does not (p. 127). If fancy does not awaken emotion, then fancy is ruled out of literature by the author's essential definition, and that would result in absurd consequences fatal to his theory.

Professor Winchester's good taste keeps him from the conclusions to which his theory, logically followed out, might lead. He has no sympathy with the school of literature or poetry which makes the spinal thrill the final test of poetic and literary excellence. A professor in one of our large universities subscribes to the theory of the spinal thrill. (*Bookman,* Oct., 1917, p. 133.) The extreme statement of the theory is found in the preface of *At a Venture,* a volume of poems issued by Blackwell, Oxford (1917). " The wisest know that poetry is a human utterance, at once inevitable and unforced, and leave it at that. This much is certain: Reason has no part in it. There is no Muse

of Logic.   Feeling, which of its essence de-
fies logical limitation, is the be-all and end-all
of Poetry.   Ultimately, perhaps, the spinal
thrill is the surest working test."   How far
this statement is from Wordsworth's description of poetry as the " breath and finer
spirit of all knowledge " and from Pater's,
" All beauty is in the long run only fineness
of truth or what we call expression, the finer
accommodation of speech to that vision
within ! "

The earlier critics did not neglect emotions
in their criticism of literature and of poetry,
but Keble was probably the first who made
the feelings and emotions so prominent a
factor in poetry, which in his Oxford lectures
he described as a relief of the emotions.   It
may have been due to these lectures that
Newman added a note to his essay on Aristotle's poetics, making " the moving of the
affections through the imagination " the
function and aim of poetry.   With Keble
emotions were the efficient cause; with Newman the affections, not a happy term, seem to
be the final cause of poetry.

All this confusion about the emotions in
poetry and fine art arises from a neglect or
obscuring of the distinction between the appetitive emotions and the cognitive or
esthetic emotions.   Balfour in a lecture,

Criticism and Beauty, given at Oxford in
1909, after a depressing and skeptical rejection of all else connected with the idea of
beauty, makes the following declaration:
" What are the esthetic emotions about.
which we have been occupied in these pages?
They are the highest members of a great
class whose common characteristic is that
they do not lead to action. It is their pecu-
liarity and their glory that they have nothing
to do with business, with the adaptation of
means to ends, with the bustle and dust of
life. . . . They are self-sufficing, and neither
point to any good beyond themselves, nor
overflow except by accident into any practical activities " (p. 41). " Here then we
have two great divisions of feeling,— the
one self-sufficing, contemplative, not looking
beyond its boundaries, nor essentially
prompting to action; the other lying at the
root of conduct, always having some external reference, supplying the immediate
motive for all the actions of mankind. Of
highest value in the contemplative division
is the feeling of beauty; of highest value
in the active division is the feeling of
love " (p. 45).

Balfour states here at length what St.
Thomas puts succinctly and comprehensively:
" Good has the nature of an end or final

cause; beauty that of a formal cause " (S. I, 5, 4). " Beauty regards knowledge " (*ibid.*). " It belongs to beauty to satisfy by its sight and contemplation " (S. I, 2, 27, 1). This is the teaching of all scholastic philosophers from his time down to Coffey's *Ontology* and Mercier's *Ontologie*.

The neglect or obscuring of the fundamental distinction between the emotions which are of the will and those which are of the mind permeates Winchester's *Principles of Literary Criticism* and much recent criticism. Taste and a subconscious feeling for the truth keeps most critics from the spinal thrill absurdity, but it is unfortunate that this clear and fundamental distinction should in the slightest way be obscured.

Esthetic emotions differ from other emotions in faculty, in origin, in nature. To desire a fruit, to hope for it, to joy in its possession or grieve for its loss, these are emotions which are not esthetic. Hope, desire, fear, joy, sadness and the like are tendencies towards good or away from evil and are modifications of the primal emotions of love and hate. Even disinterested love begins in appetitive tendency and when it reaches the stage of so called benevolence, it is still tending towards good but now towards a higher and unselfish good. On the

other hand, esthetic emotions are not characterized by that outward tendency to an
end. Interest, taste, wonder, mental delight, awe, inspiration, enthusiasm are some
of the esthetic emotions, although not all of
these terms have the precise meaning and
definite use which belongs to the correspond-
ing terms of the other class of emotions. In
truth, the specific kinds of esthetic emotions
have not been as definitely determined or as
carefully differentiated as the kinds of emotions awakened by good or evil. Yet experience testifies that to call to imagination the
vision of a fruit, to contemplate it, to admire
shape, color or other beauties, may be just as
free from desire, hope and other species of
love and hate as the contemplation of a
painted or sculptured fruit would be. The
esthetic emotions belong to the faculty of
knowing, which is not self-seeking. The
other emotions belong to the will and appetite which are of their very nature and always must be self-seeking. Only good, or
an end, can actuate will and appetite, and
beauty, as such, has not, in the words of
Aquinas, " the nature of an end."

What has led some astray is the fact that
literature and all arts may present emotions
as their subject matter just as they present
persons and actions. " Even dancing," says

Aristotle, "imitates character, emotion and action." Such emotions are the material objects of art, and are no more its formal object than character or action constitute such a formal object. Certain specific emotions are essential to certain species of literature, as fear and terror to tragedy, but these emotions are essential to the species not to poetry in general, anymore than because to shave the beard is the specific work of the razor as distinguished from other knives, therefore all knives cut beards. In Aristotle's teaching it is the "imitation" which is the essential note of art; it is the "imitation" which gives the artistic pleasure; it is the "imitation" which by transferring nature to another universe through the different mediums of words, sounds, pigments and solids, generalizes the artist's subject, frees it from actuality, puts characters, actions and emotions into a sound world or color world or shape world or word world where appetitive emotions are released and awakened but are robbed of their personal application by being transferred through imitation to another sphere. The emotion of fear is as innocuous for the spectator of a tragedy as the emotion of desire for the admirer of a painted apple. "Imitation" is originally a dramatic term and was transferred from the stage to all arts. Dramatization or staging would give the various suggestions of the term better than imitation. Whatever be Aristotle's full meaning, it is in dramatization that he places the essential note of all arts.

Aristotle in his *Poetics* (XIV, 3) gives a sentence which illustrates his teaching and adequately discriminates the three elements here discussed. "And since the pleasure which the poet should afford is that which comes from pity and fear through imitation, it is evident that this quality must be impressed upon the incidents." (*Butcher's transl.*) Here, the poet is the tragic poet; pleasure is the esthetic emotion, the subjective effects " from (ἀπό) pity and fear " denotes the subject matter of his tragic art; and "through (διά) imitation" sets forth the cause. Aristotle does not say " quality " in the original text; he uses the indefinite τοῦτο. " This poetic effect is to be brought about in the incidents," states Aristotle's meaning fairly.

This digression to Aristotle has taken us away from the main question, which is, that esthetic emotions are essentially different from the emotions which lead to action. Esthetic emotions are caused by beauty, are cognitive and unselfish in nature and are connected with the senses, imagination and mind, whereas the common emotions of love and hate with all their species are awakened by good and evil, are self-seeking emotions and are connected with the spiritual or corporal appetite.

The earlier criticism which judged all literature and art in terms of the imagination and the later criticism which judges all literature and art in terms of emotions are both right but are both defective through lack of definition. The term, imagination, should be restricted to its usual meaning, the material faculty which stores up the impressions of the senses and images objects in their absence. The imagination works always in union with the mind but is not the mind. In art the imagination is important because the beauty of art is embodied in a concrete medium, and the vivid imagining of the artist's product precedes, accompanies and perfects his work. The term, emotion, should likewise be carefully distinguished into its two kinds. When we agree upon what is meant by these terms and keep to that agreement, literary and artistic criticism will be greatly benefited.

XVIII

ORIGINALITY BY IMITATION

XVIII

ORIGINALITY BY IMITATION

PROBABLY nothing is so much in demand in the world as originality. Originality is interesting because novelty interests through the freshness of its appeal, and originality might be styled individual novelty. That is why at this very moment there are versifiers and novelists and essayists and writers of every class, vainly striving to shift the various scenes before their mind's eye into some new and strange picture. Advertisers, purveyors of amusement, preachers, teachers, merchants and mechanics, scientists and inventors, honest men and rogues, are all endeavoring to compass originality, in hope of influencing the great public for their own immediate purposes. The intense rivalry between newspapers and magazines to keep abreast or even ahead of the times will be found to spring from the same desire. It is clear, then, that a glorious triumph awaits him who can bring originality

out of the regions of chance and place it in
the certain reach of all.

Many have attempted, with varying de-
grees of success, to reduce originality to rule
or to define it more accurately. A writer
in *Literature* says, " The matter of a literary
work of art may come from nature, from
life, from another book, while the form is
created by the author." The specific cause
of originality is here set forth, but is amounts
to nothing more than what we have heard
so often, *non nova sed nove.* Hartley
Coleridge says, " There are few synonyms in
any language; but there is in the English a
perfect synonym to the word original: it is
— the scarcely less abused word — natural."
He transfers the discussion from original to
natural and at the same time admits paren-
thetically that he has not lessened the difficulties. He has, however, given a test, a
standard, by which all the counterfeits of
originality may be detected. The same author goes on to say that " every sentiment
that proceeds from the heart, every thought
that emanates from the individual mind or
is suggested by personal observation is original, though, in all probability, it has been
thought and felt a thousand times before."
Here is a more definite statement tracing
originality more clearly to its source.

To the same effect is the opinion of Mabie:
"Personality is the divinest thing in the
world, because it is the only creative thing;
the only power that can bring to material
already existent a new idea of order and
form." The subject matter may then be
old if the presentation be individual and personal, but how the subject matter is to become personal we are not told. Mabie
quotes from Goethe: "People are always
talking about originality, but what do they
mean?. As soon as we are born, the world
begins to work upon us, and this goes on to
the end. And, after all, what can we call
our own except energy, strength and will?
If I could give an account of all I owe to
great predecessors and contemporaries, there
would be a small balance in my favor."

It is evident that these words but reiterate the fact that what we write of is, and
must be, borrowed in many ways. They do
not enlighten us how the borrowings become
personal property; for all borrow, few im-
press their individuality on what they have
received. Hazlitt affirms most of what has
already been stated, but puts the question in
a new light when he writes, "Originality is
the seeing nature differently from others and
yet as it is in itself," and again, "This is
the test and triumph of originality, not to

show us what has never been, but to point
out to us what is before our eyes and under
our feet, though we have had no suspicion of
its existence, for want of sufficient strength
of intuition, of determined grasp of mind, to
seize and retain it."

All these opinions are undoubtedly of
great help to us, if not positively at least
negatively. They give us rules and direc-
tions which will enable us to start on the
right path and avoid many of the pitfalls
which lie thick along the way to originality.
We have but to recall the epithets applied to
these pitfalls and they will bring to mind
many a dismal failure. What a history is
conveyed in the terms, novel, fanciful, affected, odd, eccentric, grotesque and sensational! The associations which surround
" sensational " would fill a volume by themselves.

It may also be said of the opinions cited
that they agree to the extent of not requiring
originality in the subject matter. We may
transform what we acquire or inherit, but
inherit or acquire we must, and cannot create except in a metaphorical sense. Just as
the energy which does all the work in this
world is always the same in quantity as it has
ever been, but is variously transformed from
coal into heat, from heat into steam, from

steam into momentum, from momentum into collision, so the great body of thought, which is our heritage from antiquity, undergoes many a change as it passes down the ages.

It is, of course, a commonplace in philosophy that man acquires everything by imitation. By imitation we first learned to talk, and to gesticulate and to walk. As time went on, these actions, because of the texture of chord and muscle, by reflection and practice and habit, became individual. What is true of bodily actions is true as well in matters of the mind. We are not born with ready-made ideas. We must acquire them; we must bring them through the senses; we must get them from outside, and for the most part from books.

Here, however, we meet with a difficulty. Hartley Coleridge denies that books promote originality, and asserts that original knowledge is to be gained from life and observation. The statement has much truth in it, but we cannot now stop to separate the true from the false. But is it a fact that there is no life or observation of nature in books? What are the thoughts, the hopes, the fears, the emotions, the passions of man, but life, and the most intense and truest life? Is not the nature of man, if no other nature, set forth for our most earnest observation in the best books of all times?   The ancients, we believe, had the right theory and practice when they subordinated nature to man. The full meaning, we also believe, of the word, nature, will not be grasped, except as it is ordained to man, and interpreted by him. The writers of the world reveal to us this interpretation, and teach us how to look on nature and understand it.

If ideas are derived in great part from books, it remains to consider what is the method by which those ideas become original.   Cardinal Newman defines originality as the power of abstracting for one's self. "Our opinions," he says, "are commonly derived from education and society.   Common minds transmit as they receive, good and bad, true and false; minds of original talent feel a continual propensity to investigate subjects and strike out views for themselves — so that even old and established truths do not escape modification and accidental change when subjected to this process of mental digestion."   To become, therefore, original, passive reception of truths is not enough.   There must be investigation, there must be expeditions in various branching ways.   We must strike out views, we must cut innumerable facets on the rough

diamond of truth, transmitted to us from
others.   There must be a mental digestion,
the substance of the thought must be assimi-
lated.   Thus it will become personal and individual.

Let us remove here an opinion which
would perhaps prove misleading.   Reading
has been defended and insisted on, but it
must be borne in mind that if all the books
in the world were read, transferred to notes
and committed to memory, originality would
not be the outcome, were the work to stop
there.   It is thinking, not reading, which
produces originality.   To read is a necessary
means; to think is the all-important cause.
To champion thought is to wage a hard battle, because thought is labor.   But we must
think, each one for himself; we must have,
according to Hazlitt, that quality of mind
" into which the quality of the object sinks
deepest, where it finds most cordial welcome,
is perceived to its utmost extent, and where
again it forces its way out from the fulness
with which it has taken possession of the
mind of the student."

By such mental work the imagination is
warmed, and it is commonly agreed that the
imagination is an all-important factor in
originality.   When the thought is turned
over and over again in the mind, its different

phases present themselves, their connection
with each other and with other thoughts is
made manifest, various analogies are suggested, new combinations are formed, a development along given lines begins to grow
and branch, here losing itself in darkness,
there stretching on in vistas under brighter
light.   Have you ever seen a jumbled mass
of iron filings range in line, as obediently as
soldiers, under the unseen spell of magnet-
ism?   You had then a picture of the way
ideas group themselves along new lines, under repeated applications of the power of
the mind.   Have you watched the electro-
lysis of water?   Let the influence of mind
work on the commonest of ideas, and in the
agitation some new combination will result.
Subject the oldest ideas to the steady gaze
of the mind, and newly made crystals of
brilliant truth will gradually evolve.

By thought, therefore, we turn information into knowledge; we assimilate the substance of what we have received.   What was
foreign becomes native; what was common
becomes personal; what was strange becomes
familiar.   Habit grows into second nature.
We observe our own thoughts.   Note-taking from others does not promote originality, quite the contrary; but note-taking from
our own minds produces original thought.

We have thought for ourselves, and the thought is colored with self.   The ideas become natural to us.   We say what seems to us to be known by everybody, and we are surprised to find that we are original.   The ease of original composition, the absence of all traces of workmanship, the freshness of life without pretence or false gloss, are all so many witnesses to the completion with which the matter has been domiciled in the mind.   Can we not, however, be more definite than merely to say, " Think, and you will be original? "   Are there no lines along which our thinking should go?

Man is ever the same.   The Homeric hero never spoke through a telephone or rode on an electric car; he never read a newspaper or smoked a cigarette, but he had the same heart, the same impulses, the same virtues and failings as we have.   The same considerations which moved him move us. If, therefore, we would touch and influence men, we must use the same means, essentially, as have been powerful hitherto.   The underlying principles which make the heart glow and the mind active, though they vary accidentally in their presentation, will ever be fundamentally the same.   If, then, after familiarizing ourselves with the ideas of an author, we separate what is essential from

what is merely accidental, if we place our
esteem where it is due, we shall find the
fundamental thought " force its way out
from the fulness with which it has taken possession of the mind."   If we admire what is
really worthy of admiration, if we have right
principles guiding us in what we think much
of, if, in a word, we comprehend why one
thing is good and why another is not, we
shall in our imitation — for imitate we
must — reproduce, not any modifications
which previous writers may have brought
about, but essential truths, as they are perceived by ourselves, and in so doing we shall
be original.   Surely, he who knows the secret of another's power, the real cause of
his success, neglecting unessential details,
will put that cause into action, and will produce like results.

An example will make this process clear.
He who thinks he will be well dressed because he has the same cloth or the same cut
as some one whom he admires, makes, of
course, a mistake.   He may have the exact
reproduction of another's apparel, and yet
because he has not understood why his ideal
was well dressed, he may succeed in turning
himself into a clothier's model, but will fail
in his efforts at elegance.   How much different the result would be if he perceived the

principles upon which his friend selected his
articles of dress. In that case he would
imitate his friend by putting his principles of
taste into practice, and though the material
and style might be altogether different, the
effect would be tasteful and original. A
great author, too, will have his followers.
Some will be of small intellect and little application. They will fasten with joy on a
turn of a sentence or a trick of style, and, of
course, in striving to imitate write parodies.
Others will think their favorite author is
powerful because of a peculiar vocabulary
or dialect, and we shall have reams of unin-
telligible provincialisms. How many copied
Tennyson's peculiarities, how few really imitated him! It was Tennyson's misfortune
to have had peculiarities of vocabulary, of
style and of metre, and his short-sighted admirers, failing to see the fitness of all this in
Tennyson, thought to win renown by carefully alliterating or by doubling their adjectives or by using old English words and lus-
cious sounds and rimes. They gave us parodies, not original poems.

> They lyricked hopes and tongued sweet lays,
> And held it very truth, I ween,
> To weave a subtle shot-silk sheen,
> With warp and woof of metric maze.

Cardinal Newman, on the other hand, has told us that if he had any model it was Cicero, and yet, who can detect any of the mannerisms of Cicero in his style. That he admired Cicero on principle, and so succeeded in imitating him with originality, is evident from his acute criticism of the excellence and defects of Cicero's style.

It is, perhaps, rather unfortunate that what has been written here cannot be exhibited as an example of the theory expounded, but the conclusions can lay no claim to originality. We have been endeavoring to interpret what has been well said before. It may be stated too pompously, but it surely will prove helpful and suggestive. We refer to a passage occurring in Samuel Taylor Coleridge's *Biographia Litteraria.* We call attention especially to the most suggestive, though apparently paradoxical, epigram with which the citation closes. "In energetic minds truth soon changes by domestication into power; and from directing in the discrimination and appraisal of the product, becomes influencive in the production. (To admire on principle is the only way to imitate without loss of originality." Coleridge owes this thought to Reynolds who delivered his Lectures on Painting in 1774, and in the lecture on imitation makes the following statements: " Invention is one of the great marks of genius, but if we consult experience, we shall find that it is by being conversant with the inventions of others that we learn to invent as by reading the thoughts of others we learn to think." " We must not content ourselves with merely admiring and relishing; we must enter into the principles on which the work is wrought; these do not swim on the superficies and consequently are not open to the superficial observer." " Find out the latent cause of conspicuous beauties and from them form principles." " What is learned in this manner from the works of others becomes really our own." Coleridge has condensed the truths of Reynolds and put them in a pointed way, and both agree that originality may be learned from the masters who are original.

XIX

EXERCISES FOR THE IMAGINATION

XIX

EXERCISES FOR THE IMAGINATION [1]

GENERAL topics often discussed do not reach into the writer's sluggish imagination and force it to display its hidden treasures, but if an old topic is attacked on a new and definite point, it is likely to enliven the writer and to key up all his faculties to full action.

I. LIMIT THE TOPIC

Limit the topic to something specific and particular; present it as a problem for question, debate, or refutation; state it in a comparison or metaphor which permits detailed development; embody the topic dramatically in a character of a scene; enliven it with humor.

A trite subject like the *Duty of Gratitude* may receive fresh handling under one of the following topics:

[1] The substance of this chapter is taken from the author's *Model English,* Book II (Allyn and Bacon).

Specific:

Gratitude on a railroad train.
Thanks due to teacher, etc.
Grateful actors, audiences.
Is gratitude displayed in word only?
Testamentary gratitude.

Problematic:

What is the true test of gratitude?
When is it hardest to be grateful?
Isn't gratitude a mere formality?
What is the best way to show gratitude?
Is gratitude more necessary than kindness?
Who are more grateful, boys or girls?
Do teachers or parents deserve more gratitude?
When is gratitude born and when does it die?

Metaphorical:

Gratitude, the lubricant of life's friction.
Bankrupts in the currency of gratitude.
The music of " Thank you."
Justice of the heart.
When favors call, is gratitude at home?

Dramatic:

The finest gratitude I ever saw.
The worst ingratitude I know of.
The history of a single " Thank you."
   (Cf. Addison's *History of a Shilling*.) .
I Thankyou, a good friend of mine.
   (Cf. Goldsmith's *Man in Black*.)

Humorous:

Is gratitude a lively sense of favors to come?

Places not yet discovered by gratitude.
> (A street-car conductor in Omaha said
> "Thank you" on receiving the fare.)

How to be successfully ungrateful.
> (Cf. Lang's *How to Fail in Literature*.)

Gratitude and civilization. (A savage tribe is
said to have no word for "Thank you";
the natives say, "Do it again.")

Dunning for gratitude. ("If a man does you
a favor, he follows you with a tomahawk all
your life."— New England saying.)

Wanted — a Ford for quantity production of
grateful hearts.

A new Burbank flower, the thankusir.

II. DEFINE A STATEMENT

A statement to which every one would immediately agree, sends no challenge to the writer's powers or to the reader's attention, as, Columbus was a great man. Make the statement actual, novel and challenging, and the imagination will respond.

Actual:

There are worlds still to be discovered with the
courage of Columbus.

The spirit of Columbus should be our inspiration.

A Columbus should be governor of our State.

The life of Columbus must be read by every
American.

Our city should have a Columbus pageant.

How could we educate a Columbus to-day?

Novel:

How Columbus could have failed.

The sunshine and shadows of the great sailor.

What would Columbus say to this audience?

The failure of success should be the epitaph of Columbus.

America should be called Columbia.

Was the discovery of America Columbus' greatest deed?

Challenging:

What was the leading quality of Columbus' soul?

Columbus or Washington, who deserved greater gratitude?

Columbus is the ideal sailor of history.

What one of Columbus' virtues led him to discover America?

. Was Columbus a better mariner than manager of men?

Could Columbus help discovering America?

Was Columbus more honored in his foes or in his friends?

III.   DWELL ON THE PICTURES OF POETRY

The following passages will serve as material for the exercise of imagining described in Chapter XVI.   How would you picture these and other like scenes if you were an artist?

There at the foot of yonder nodding beech,
That wreathes its old fantastic root so high.
                         —GRAY: *Elegy.*

I warmed both hands before the fire of life;
It sinks, and I am ready to depart.
    — LANDOR: *Seventy-fifth Birthday.*

I feel like one who treads alone
 Some banquet-hall deserted,
Whose lights are fled, whose garlands dead,
 And all but he departed.
    — MOORE: *Oft in the Stilly Night.*

Full many a glorious morning have I seen
Flatter the mountain tops with sovereign eye,
Kissing with golden face the meadows green,
Gilding pale streams with heavenly alchemy.
    — SHAKESPEARE: *Sonnets.*

And if I should live to be
The last leaf upon the tree
 In the spring,
Let them smile, as I do now,
At the old forsaken bough
 Where I cling.
    — HOLMES: *The Last Leaf.*

And bead by bead I tell
The Rosary of my years;
From a cross to a cross they lead; 'tis well,
And they're blessed with a blessing of tears.

Better a day of strife
Than a century of sleep.
Give me instead of a long stream of life
The tempests and tears of the deep.
    — RYAN: *The Rosary of My Tears.*

That time of year thou mayst in me behold
When yellow leaves, or none, or few, do hang
Upon those boughs that shake against the cold,
Bare ruin'd choirs, where late the sweet birds sang.
> — SHAKESPEARE: *Sonnets.*

Ah, distinctly I remember it was in the bleak
    December,
And each separate dying ember wrought its ghost
    upon the floor.
> — POE: *The Raven.*

I make the netted sunbeam dance
    Against my sandy shallows.
> — TENNYSON: *The Brook.*

Thy soul was like a star and dwelt apart.
> — WORDSWORTH: *Milton.*

Comes a vapor from the margin blackening over
    heath and holt,
Cramming all the blast before it, in its breast a
    thunderbolt.
> — TENNYSON: *Locksley Hall.*

Men whose lives ran on like rivers of woodland,
Darkened by shadows of earth but reflecting an
    image of heaven.
> — LONGFELLOW: *Evangeline.*

IV.   PUT THE CONCRETE FOR THE ABSTRACT

The abstract is the quality conceived apart
from its substance, as whiteness; the concrete
is the quality and its substance united, as a

white object, snow. The abstract can be
thought of but cannot be imagined. Every
time, therefore, that the writer goes from
the abstract to the concrete, the imagination
is exercised.

1.

The boast of heraldry, the pomp of power,
  And all that beauty, all that wealth e'er gave,
Await alike the inevitable hour;
  The paths of glory lead but to the grave.
                              — GRAY: *Elegy.*

Imagine concrete instances for all the abstract terms. Imagine the concrete pomp of
a concrete power in Greek history, in Roman
history, in your native place, etc.

2.

Sweet are the uses of adversity.
— SHAKESPEARE: *As You Like It.*

Imagine a concrete adversity with its specific use and sweetness. It is not imagining
to substitute other indefinite words, as, Helpful are the advantages of suffering. You
must picture something from history or experience.

3.

The New Testament parallel for asceticism is,
"Take up your cross daily." What are the concrete parallels in the New Testament for persever-

ance, strength of character, good example, hypocrisy, unity of Church, necessity of grace, Divine Providence, etc.?

4.

I proposed this conundrum to Father Letheby that same evening: "Why is it considered a greater crime to denounce and correct an evil than to commit it?" He looked at me as if he doubted my sanity. I put it in a more euphemistic form: "Why is success always the test of merit? To come down from the abstract to the concrete, Why is a gigantic swindler a great financier, and a poor fellow that steals a loaf of bread a felon and a thief? Why is a colossal liar a great diplomatist, and a petty prevaricator a base and ignoble fraud? Why is Napoleon a hero, and that wretched tramp an ever to be dreaded murderer? Why is Bismarck called great, though he crushed the French into a compost of blood and rags, ground them by taxation into paupers, jested at dying children, and lied most foully, and his minor imitators are dubbed criminals and thieves?"

— SHEEHAN: *My New Curate.*

SUBJECTS

Come down from the abstract to the concrete:

Fortune favors the brave.
Discretion is the better part of valor.
Dexterity comes by experience.

Familiarity breeds contempt.
Honors change manners.

5.

The most amiable of mankind may well be moved to indignation when what he has earned hardly and lent with great inconvenience to himself, for the purpose of relieving a friend in distress, is squandered with insane profusion. The real history, we have little doubt, was something like this: a letter comes to Addison, imploring help in pathetic terms, and promising reformation and speedy repayment. Poor Dick declares that he has not an inch of candle, or a bushel of coals, or credit with the butcher for a shoulder of mutton. Addison is moved. He determines to deny himself some medals which are wanting to his series of the Twelve Cæsars, to put off buying the new edition of Bayle's Dictionary, and to wear his old sword and buckles another year; in this way he manages to send a hundred pounds to his friend. The next day he calls on Steele, and finds scores of gentlemen and ladies assembled. The fiddles are playing. The table is groaning under Champagne, Burgundy, and pyramids of sweetmeats. Is it strange that a man whose kindness is thus abused should send sheriff's officers to reclaim what is due to him?
— MACAULAY: *Addison.*

Note how all the abstract indefinite terms of the first sentence are clothed in imaginative form by Macaulay in the rest of the paragraph.   Study carefully the concrete realization of each abstract original: " distress, inconvenience, profusion."

SUBJECTS

Express with a like concreteness the following abstract statements:

The privations and suffering of Washington's soldiers during the winter at Valley Forge did not cool the ardor of their patriotism.

The industry of the student will be rewarded by the approbation of the judicious and by well-merited success in life.

Political rivalry concerns itself frequently with personalities rather than with the discussion of methods of civic or national improvement.

The sublime principles of the Gospel were adapted to the capacity of the rudest listener by their concrete presentation.

6.

Burke had in the highest degree that noble faculty whereby man is able to live in the past and in the future, in the distant and in the unreal.   India and its inhabitants were not to him, as to most Englishmen, mere names and abstractions, but a real country and a real people.   The burning sun, the strange vegetation of the palm and the cocoa

tree, the ricefield, the tank, the huge trees, older
than the Mogul empire, under which the village
crowds assemble, the thatched roof of the peasant's
hut, the rich tracery of the mosque where the imaum
prays with his face to Mecca, the drums, and the
banners, and gaudy idols, the devotee swinging in
the air, the graceful maiden, with the pitcher on her
head, descending the steps to the river-side, the
black faces, the long beards, the yellow streaks of
sect, the turbans and the flowing robes, the spears
and the silver maces, the elephants with their cano-
pies of state, the gorgeous palanquin of the prince,
and the close litter of the noble lady, all these
things were to him as the objects amidst which his
own life had been passed, as the objects which lay
on the road between Beaconsfield and St. James's
Street. All India was present to the eye of his
mind, from the halls where suitors laid gold and
perfumes at the feet of sovereigns to the wild moor
where the gypsy camp was pitched, from the bazar,
humming like a bee-hive with the crowd of buyers
and sellers, to the jungle where the lonely courier
shakes his bunch of iron rings to scare away the
hyænas. He had just as lively an idea of the insur-
rection at Benares as of Lord George Gordon's
riots, and of the execution of Nuncomar as of the
execution of Dr. Dodd. Oppression in Bengal was
to him the same thing as oppression in the streets
of London.

— MACAULAY: *Warren Hastings.*

How would these concrete details appear
as " abstractions "?

Set forth in concrete details:
A poet's vision of spring.
An enthusiast's knowledge of Dickens, etc.
A great painter's acquaintance with nature.
A great man's mastery of his trade (ships, machinery, steel, etc.).
A girl's dream of fashions and finery.

7.

What is it, sir, that makes the great difference between country and country? Not the exuberance of soil; not the mildness of climate; not mines, nor havens, nor rivers. These things are indeed valuable when put to their proper use by human intelligence; but human intelligence can do much without them; and they without human intelligence can do nothing. They exist in the highest degree in regions of which the inhabitants are few and squalid and barbarous and naked and starving; while on sterile rocks, amidst unwholesome marshes, and under inclement skies, may be found immense populations, well fed, well lodged, well clad, well governed. Nature meant Egypt and Sicily to be the gardens of the world. They once were so. Is it anything in the earth or in the air that makes Scotland more prosperous than Egypt, that makes Holland more prosperous than Sicily? No; it was the Scotchman that made Scotland; it was the Dutchman that made Holland. Look at North America. Two centuries ago the sites on which now arise mills and hotels and banks and colleges and churches and the senate houses of flourishing commonwealths,

were deserts abandoned to the panther and the bear.
What had made the change? Was it the rich
mould, or the redundant rivers? No; the prairies
were as fertile, the Ohio and the Hudson were as
broad and as full then as now. Was the improvement the effect of some great transfer of capital
from the Old World to the New? No; the emi-
grants generally carried out with them no more
than a pittance; but they carried out the English
heart, and head, and arm; and the English heart
and head and arm turned the wilderness into corn-
field and orchard, and the huge trees of the prime-
val forest into cities and fleets.

  — MACAULAY: *The Ten Hours Law.*

The substance of the passage might be
freely stated in this abstract fashion: " It
is not the richness of nature but human intelligence which gives to a barren wilderness
prosperity and fruitfulness."

Note how all the ideas are made definite,
specific, and concrete as the speaker proves
his point. Make the thoughts in the exercises as concrete as you can.

SUBJECTS

Be definite and concrete:

The tales in the Arabian Nights are store-
houses of bewildering dreams.

Nature in America offers varied attractions for lovers of beautiful and sublime scenery.

The history of the United States reveals a new experience in the forming of one nation from various nationalities.

It is not natural endowment but persevering application which gives success in literature.

> The glory that was Greece
> And the grandeur that was Rome.
> — POE: *To Helen.*

V.   PUT THE PARTICULAR FOR THE GENERAL

The definition, say, of a house, as conceived by the mind is general and true of any and every house; the picture of a house formed in the imagination at one moment will be of a particular size and shape.   To go, therefore, from a general statement to a particular is an exercise of the imagination.   It is usual with good writers to follow up a general assertion with a particular instance by way of proof or example.

Note how Ruskin does this within one sentence:

Let the reader consider seriously what he would give at any moment to have the power of arresting the fairest scenes, those which so often rise before him only to vanish; to stay the cloud in its fading, the leaf in its trembling, and the shadows in their

changing; to bid the fitful foam be fixed upon the
river and the ripples be everlasting on the lake.
                                        — *Modern Painters.*

The general terms are " arresting," " fairest scenes," " rise to vanish."   What are the
particular terms for each?

By an ironical insistence on obvious particulars Arnold gently ridicules the conveniences invented by his so-called " Philistines."

How Philistinism has augmented the comforts
and conveniences of life for us! Doors that open,
windows that shut, locks that turn, razors that
shave, coats that wear, watches that go, and a thousand more such good things, are the inventions of
the Philistines.
                                        — *Celtic Literature.*

1.

Proverbs are general truths drawn from
particular instances. What particular instances do you imagine for these proverbs?

More haste, less speed.
Procrastination is the thief of time.
Evil communications corrupt good manners.
Eternal vigilance is the price of liberty.
Necessity is the mother of invention.

2.

Imagine particular beauties with particular

joys and read the opening lines of Keats'
Endymion to find what he imagined.

A thing of beauty is a joy forever.

3.

Supply new pictures for general headings
such as cartoonists employ:

" When a feller needs a friend."
" The worst is yet to come."
" Ain't that a grand and glorious feeling? "
" And then I woke up."
" The thrill that comes once in a lifetime."

4.

Covetousness of riches is folly.

Imagine a particular instance and compare
Luke xii. 13–21.

5.

That loss is common would not make
My own less bitter, rather more;
Too common! Never morning wore
To evening but some heart did break.

Imagine particular losses and then compare Tennyson's *In Memoriam*, VI. For
other general and particular statements see
Tennyson's *Amphion, The Voyage of Mael-
dune.*

6.

Then where, o'er two bright havens,
  The towers of Corinth frown;
Where the gigantic King of Day
  On his own Rhodes looks down;
Where soft Orontes murmurs
  Beneath the laurel shades;
Where Nile reflects the endless length
  Of dark-red colonnades;
Where in the still deep water,
  Sheltered from waves and blasts,
Bristles the dusky forest
  Of Byrsa's thousand masts;
Where fur-clad hunters wander
  Amidst the northern ice;
Where through the sand of morning-land
  The camel bears the spice;
Where Atlas flings his shadow
  Far o'er the western foam,—
Shall be great fear on all who hear
  The mighty name of Rome.
    — MACAULAY: *Lays of Ancient Rome.*

" Everywhere shall be fear of Rome " is
the thought which is developed imaginatively
by enumerating choice particulars.

SUBJECTS

Imagine in detail with apt circumstances:
  Cities or mountains or bodies of water
(crossing America, or other country in an
airplane).

Ports touched at in a voyage around the world.

Books of the library or characters in them.

Streams or cities of your state.

Streets and parks of your city.

7.

Wherever we go all over the earth, it is the solitary Briton, the London agent, or the Milordos, who is walking restlessly about, abusing the natives, and raising a colossus, or setting the Thames on fire, in the East or the West. He is on the top of the Andes or in the diving-bell in the Pacific, or taking notes at Timbuctoo, or grubbing at the Pyramids, or scouring over the Pampas, or acting as prime minister to the king of Dahomey, or smoking the pipe of friendship with the Red Indians, or hutting at the Pole. No one can say beforehand what will come of these various specimens of the independent, self-governing, self-reliant Englishman. Sometimes failure, sometimes opening for trade, scientific discoveries, or political aggrandizements.

— NEWMAN: *Who's To Blame?*

"The various specimens of the self-reliant Englishman" are detailed with fine imagination and with humorous exaggeration.

SUBJECTS

Enumerate:

The efforts of a tramp to avoid work.

The various industries of an energetic
farmer.
The worries of an anxious mother.
The duties of a policeman.
The wandering of a stray dog.
The adventures of a dime.

8.

Then too may come the dull philosopher of the
age to rebuke our folly, our want of sense, our in-
discretion; and proclaim that patriotism, a wild and
glittering passion, has died out — that it could not
coincide with civilization, the steam-engine, and free
trade.   It is false!   The virtue that gave to Pagan-
ism its dazzling luster — to barbarism its redeeming
trait — to Christianity its heroic form — is not
dead.   It still lives to preserve, to console, to sanc-
tify humanity.   It has its altar in every clime,—
its worship and festivities.   On the heathered hills
of Scotland, the sword of Wallace is yet a bright
tradition.   The genius of France, in the brilliant
literature of the day, pays its enthusiastic homage
to the piety and heroism of the young maid of Or-
leans.   In her new senate hall, England bids her
sculptor place, among the effigies of her greatest
sons, the images of her Hampden and her Russell.
In the gay and graceful capital of Belgium, the dar-
ing hand of Geefs has reared a monument, full of
glorious meaning, to the three hundred martyrs of
the revolution.   By the soft, blue waters of Lake
Lucerne stands the chapel of William Tell.   On
the anniversary of his revolt and victory, across

those waters, as they glitter in the July sun, skim the light boats of the allied cantons. From the prows hang the banners of the republic, and as they near the sacred spot, the daughters of Lucerne chant the hymns of their old, poetic land. Then bursts forth the glad Te Deum, and heaven hears again the voice of that wild chivalry of the mountains which, five centuries since, pierced the white eagle of Vienna and flung it bleeding on the rocks of Uri. At Innsbruck, in the black side of the old cathedral, the peasant of the Tyrol kneels before the statue of Andreas Hofer. In the defiles and valleys of the Tyrol, who forgets the day on which he fell within the walls of Mantua? It is a festive day all through his quiet, noble land. In that old cathedral his inspiring memory is recalled amid the pageantries of the altar — his image appears in every house — his victories and virtues are proclaimed in the songs of the people. Sir, shall we not join in the glorious worship, and here in this Island — anointed by the blood of many a good and gallant man — shall we not have the faith, the duties, the festivities of patriotism? You discard the weapons of these heroic men — do not discard their virtues.

— MEAGHER: *Placehunting.*

This passage comes at the close of a speech. Meagher was a fiery and ornate speaker and though the wealth of imagination shown here is not often required, yet its study is helpful. The feeling of sincerity of

the speaker and his taste keep him from
excess. "Patriotism has its worship and
festivities in every clime," is the general
statement.

SUBJECTS

Imagine particular details:
The heroism of American soldiers.
The glories of literature.
The adventurous spirit of the world's dis-
coverers.
The perseverance of the great inventors.
The wonders of science and scientists.
The apostles of Christianity.

VI.   PUT A SIGNIFICANT PART FOR THE
WHOLE

The whole is often vague and indefinite or
has lost color through much use. For these
reasons, it does not appeal to the imagination.
The choice of a significant or typical part
gives a fresh view and by imagining a part
only, the whole is often pictured more effectively. "If thou see a man of understanding, go to him early in the morning and let
thy foot wear the steps of his door." Ecclus.
vi, 36. The latter part of this advice would
be less attractive and imaginative if it read:
Do you spend a long time at his house.

1.

It is related that a lost traveler came in sight of a scaffold and cried, " Now I know I have arrived at civilization." Some one has said that the civilization of a country may be measured by the amount of soap it uses. A scaffold and the use of soap are parts of civilization humorously suggestive of the whole. What would you imagine as suggestive of education, politeness, gratitude, humility, anger, democracy, autocracy, slavery, want, etc. ?

2.

On this question of principle, while actual suffering was yet afar off, our fathers raised their flag against a power, to which, for purposes of foreign conquest and subjugation, Rome in the height of her glory is not to be compared; a power which has dotted over the surface of the whole globe with her possessions and military posts, whose morning drumbeat, following the sun and keeping company with the hours, circles the earth with one continuous and broken strain of the martial airs of England.
— WEBSTER: *Presidential Protest.*

The world-wide power of England is expressed in one significant part, the drum-beat, circling the world. Imagine a significant feature to express: the danger of the great ocean to Columbus, the difficulties of the journey to explorers of the poles, the deadliness of a plague, the horrors of a fire or flood, the influence of the press, the might of the labor movement, the place of the Church in history.

3.

Leave to the soft Campanian
  His baths and his perfumes;
Leave to the sordid race of Tyre
  Their dyeing-vats and looms;
Leave to the sons of Carthage
  The rudder and the oar:
Leave to the Greek his marble Nymphs
  And scrolls of wordy lore.
Thine, Roman, is the pilum;
  Roman, the sword is thine,
The even trench, the bristling mound,
  The legion's ordered line;
And thine the wheels of triumph,
  Which with their laurelled train
Move slowly up the shouting streets
  To Jove's eternal fane.
  — MACAULAY: *Lays of Ancient Rome.*

The poet picks out traits characteristic of the various nations. Choose characteristic traits of the several professions, doctors, lawyers; painters, etc.; of various states or cities; of various modern nations; of various streets in your native place; of parts of the house, etc.

4.

Or from the bridge I leaned to hear
  The milldam rushing down with noise
And see the minnows everywhere
  In crystal eddies glance and poise.
— TENNYSON: *The Miller's Daughter.*

"Glance," the swift dart of the minnow reflecting the sunlight from its scales, and " poise," the quivering pause before a new dart, are two characteristic acts of a minnow.

What actions would you choose as characteristic of a cat or kitten, of a dog, a horse in the pasture, a snake, a bird in the air, a butterfly, a fly, a locomotive, soldiers, sailors, tramps, etc.?

5.

From every warlike city
  That boasts the Latin name,
Foredoomed to dogs and vultures,
  That gallant army came;
From Setia's purple vineyards,
  From Norba's ancient wall,
From the white streets of Tusculum,
  The proudest town of all;
From where the Witch's Fortress
  O'erhangs the dark-blue seas;
From the still glassy lake that sleeps
  Beneath Aricia's trees, . . .
From the drear banks of Ufens,
  Where flights of marsh-fowl play,

And buffaloes lie wallowing
  Through the hot summer's day;
From the gigantic watch-towers,
  No work of earthly men,
Whence Cora's sentinels o'erlook
  That never rending fen;
From the Laurentian jungle,
  The wild hog's reedy home;
From the green steeps whence Anio leaps
  In floods of snow-white foam.
— MACAULAY: *Lays of Ancient Rome.*

Each spot from which the army came is given its distinctive mark. Go over a list of names, imagining some striking feature of landscape with each: nations, states, cities, towns, streets, rivers, lakes, schools, monuments.

6.

This pure creature — pure from every suspicion of even a visionary self-interest, even as she was pure in senses more obvious — never once did this holy child, as regarded herself, relax from her belief in the darkness that was traveling to meet her. She might not prefigure the very manner of her death; she saw not in vision, perhaps, the aërial altitude of the fiery scaffold, the spectators without end on every road pouring into Rouen as to a coronation, the surging smoke, the volleying flames, the hostile faces all around, the pitying eye that lurked but here and there, until nature and imperishable truth broke loose from artificial restraints; these might not be apparent through the mists of the hurrying future. But the voice that called her to death, that she heard forever.

— DE QUINCEY: *Joan of Arc.*

" The darkness " and the " manner of her death " are pictured by significant details. Contrast the other statements left without significant pictures, " nature," " imperishable truth," " artificial restraints." Could you suggest images for these terms?

SUBJECTS

Imagine by significant parts:
The death of others in history or fiction.
The child's dream of Christmas.
" The circus is coming to town! " ·
The day of graduation.
The soldier's vision.

I remember, I remember
The house where I was born.
— HOOD: *Past and Present.*

7.

We are not poorer but richer, because we have, through many ages, rested from our labor one day in seven. That day is not lost. While industry is suspended, while the plough lies in the furrow, while the Exchange is silent, while no smoke ascends from the factory, a process is going on quite as important to the wealth of nations as any process which is performed on more busy days.   Man, the machine of machines, the machine compared with which all the contrivances of the Watts and the Arkwrights are worthless, is repairing and winding up, so that he returns to his labors on the Monday with clearer intellect, with livelier spirits, with renewed corporal vigor.

— MACAULAY: *The Ten Hours Law.*

Note how in the third sentence " industry suspended " is pictured by typical parts of industry, each suspended in its particular way. What other evidences of imagination are there?   How is " process " made clear and interesting?

SUBJECTS

Imagine significant parts:
We shall profit by study.
The reader of books is not wasting his time.
Exercise has its benefits.

> Only those are crowned and sainted
> Who with grief have been acquainted.
> — LONGFELLOW: *Legend.*

8.

It is not in the language of the lawyer, or the police magistrate, that the wrongs and aspirations of an oppressed nation should be stated.   For the

pang with which it writhes,— for the passion with
which it heaves — for the chafed heart — the burning brain — the quickening pulse — the soaring soul
— there is a language quite at variance with the
grammar and the syntax of a government. It is
bold, and passionate, and generous. It often
glows with the fire of genius — it sometimes thun-
ders with the spirit of the prophet. It is tainted
with no falsehood — it is polished with no flattery.
In the desert — on the mountain — within the city
— everywhere — it has been spoken, throughout all
ages. It requires no teaching — it is the inherent
and imperishable language of humanity! Kings,
soldiers, judges, hangmen, have proclaimed it. In
pools of blood they have sought to cool and quench
this fiery tongue. They have built the prison —
they have launched the convict-ship — they have
planted the gallows tree, to warn it to be still.
The sword, the scepter, the black cap, the guillotine,
— all have failed.

— MEAGHER: *Famine and Felony.*

In this passage treating of " the language
of an oppressed nation," there are several
significant parts where one or two words expressing a whole might have been used.
What are these parts and what whole could
you substitute?

SUBJECTS

Picture apt parts in developing:
The reading of good books.

A country walk in Autumn.
Electricity in its many uses.
The variety of human amusements.
The multiplicity of children's toys.
The bewildering circus.
A day at a summer resort.

9.

But I must confess, those pictures of the mere industrial value of the Union made me profoundly sad. I look, as, beneath the skilful pencil, trait after trait leaps to glowing life, and ask at last, Is this all? Where are the nobler elements of national purpose and life? Is this the whole fruit of ages of toil, sacrifice, and thought,— those cunning fingers, the overflowing lap, labor vocal on every hillside, and commerce whitening every sea — all the dower of one haughty overbearing race? The zeal of the Puritan, the faith of the Quaker, a century of Colonial health, and then this large civilization, does it result only in a workshop,— fops melted in baths and perfumes, and men grimy with toil? Raze out, then, the Eagle from our banner, and paint instead Niagara used as a cotton-mill!

— PHILLIPS: *Lincoln's Election.*

The ideas of "industrial value" and "nobler elements" are pictured by significant parts, "fingers," "voice," "whitening sea," "Puritan," "Quaker." The whole paragraph is summed up in an imaginative epigram.

SUBJECTS

Develop imaginatively:

Don't rate a school by mere athletic supremacy but by nobler things.

Don't look merely at the difficulties of the classics but consider also their value.

A home is not precious by mere wealth but by true affection.

Remember not past pride but present weakness. (See Newman's *Lead, Kindly Light*.)

> The fault is not in our stars,
> But in ourselves that we are underlings.
> — SHAKESPEARE: *Julius Cæsar*.

10.

While this book lies on our table, we seem to be contemporaries of the writer. We are transported a hundred and fifty years back. We can almost fancy that we are visiting him in his small lodging; that we see him sitting at the old organ beneath the faded green hangings; that we can catch the quick twinkle of his eyes, rolling in vain to find the day; that we are reading in the lines of his noble countenance the proud and mournful history of his glory and his affliction. We image to ourselves the breathless silence in which we should listen to his slightest word; the passionate veneration with which we should kneel to kiss his hand and weep upon it; the earnestness with which we should endeavor to

console him, if indeed such a spirit could need con-
solation, for the neglect of an age unworthy of his
talents and his virtues; the eagerness with which we
should contest with his daughters, or with his
Quaker friend Ellwood, the privilege of reading
Homer to him, or of taking down the immortal ac-
cents which flowed from his lips.

— MACAULAY: *Milton.*

This passage comes at the close of Macaulay's Essay. He tells us he is fancying and
imagining and choosing the significant parts
which awaken pity.

SUBJECTS

*Imagine pictures for the feeling you might
excite at:*

A letter from mother.
The Liberty Bell.
A view of the Colosseum.
The relics of a martyr.
A song of childhood.
A statue of Lincoln.
The sword of Washington. (Cf. Ryan:
Sword of Lee.)

VII. LEARN TO MAKE COMPARISONS

Comparisons are usually made with objects
that fall under the senses, and the practice of
making them calls for the use of the imagina-

tion. They add much to the clearness, interest, and force of language if they are not hackneyed or strained. Hackneyed comparisons are such as have been used constantly, as " cold as ice," " shining like diamonds." Comparisons are strained if the resemblance is very slight or if too many points of resemblance are attempted. These faults are ridiculed by Newman:

The man of thought comes to the man of words; and the man of words, duly instructed in the thought, dips the pen of desire into the ink of devotedness, and proceeds to spread it over the page of desolation. Then the nightingale of affection is heard to warble to the rose of loveliness, while the breeze of anxiety plays around the brow of expectation. This is what the Easterns are said to consider fine writing.

— NEWMAN: *Literature.*

I.

Fill out these and other like phrases, which refer to the senses:

black as ——, red as ——, bitter as ——, sweet as ——, loud as ——, still as ——, fragrant as ——, rough as ——, smooth as ——, cold as ——.

Imagine new comparisons, not old ones known to every one.

2.

Fill out these expressions with pictures from home, from the street, from business, as well as from nature:

easy as ——, difficult as ——, impossible as ——, busy as ——, idle as ——, sure as ——.

See Wilstach's *Dictionary of Similes* for many used comparisons.

3.

Fill out:

Life is as swift as ——.   (Cf. Wisdom, v. 9.)

> Our tainted nature's solitary boast;
> Purer than — (one comparison)
> Brighter than — (two comparisons).
> — WORDSWORTH: *Virgin Mary.*

4.

> The lost days of my life until to-day,
> What were they, could I see them on the street
> Lie as they fell?
> — D. G. ROSSETTI: *Lost Days.*

Rossetti likens his lost days to four different things.   Can you imagine them?

> When I consider Life and its few years.
> — REESE: *Tears.*

The poet compares the few years of life to six different things.   What are they?

5.

As come the white sails of ships
　　O'er the ocean's verge;
As come the smile to the lips,
　　The foam to the surge;
So come to the poet his songs
　　All hitherward blown
From the misty realm that belongs
　　To the vast unknown.
— LONGFELLOW:　*The Poet and His Songs.*

Longfellow has nine other comparisons besides the three here.　Can you imagine some
of them?　These and the like comparisons
taken chiefly from nature and found in
poetry may serve to exercise the imagination,
but are not in place in ordinary prose where
comparisons drawn from everyday life are
better suited.　For other groups of comparisons in poetry see HALLECK:　*Marco Boz-
zaris* (*Death comes to a hero as* ——) ; MA-
CAULAY:　*Battle of Lake Regillus* (Army
attacks as ——, retreats as ——) ; BURNS:
Tam O'Shanter, 61–70 (Pleasures pass away
as —).

6.

*Imagine new pictures for the following
trite comparisons:*

A bird in the hand is worth two in the bush.
Make hay while the sun shines.

A stitch in time saves nine, etc.

A sea of upturned faces, a flood of objections, a storm of protests, etc.

To leave no stone unturned, to pave the way towards, to have a bone to pick, etc.

Dead as a door-nail, swift as lightning, sharp as a razor, etc.

A " dream," a " peach," etc.

7.

Scarcely any passages in the poems of Milton are more generally known, or more frequently repeated, than those which are little more than muster-rolls of names. They are not always more appropriate or more melodious than other names. But they are charmed names. Every one of them is the first link in a long chain of associated ideas. Like the dwelling-place of our infancy revisited in manhood, like the song of our country heard in a strange land, they produce upon us an effect wholly independent of their intrinsic value. One transports us back to a remote period of history. Another places us among the novel scenes and manners of a distant region. A third evokes all the dear classical recollections of childhood,— the schoolroom, the dog-eared Virgil, the holiday, and the prize. A fourth brings before us the splendid phantoms of chivalrous romance, the trophied lists, the embroidered housings, the quaint devices, the haunted forests, the enchanted gardens, the achievements of enamored knights, and the smiles of rescued princesses.

— MACAULAY: *Milton.*

The passage has comparisons, "link," "like the dwelling-place," "like the song," and other imaginative details. Note the "classical recollections" and "splendid phantoms."

SUBJECTS

Enumerate the concrete ideas associated with:

Your former school books.

Your haunts as a child.

Your teachers.

The towns of Belgium.

> Clime of the unforgotten brave
> Whose land from plain to mountain cave
> Was Freedom's home or Glory's grave!
> —BYRON: *The Giaour.*

8.

We are older than we were, and age is easily put out of its way. We have fewer sands in our glass to reckon upon, and we cannot brook to see them drop in endlessly succeeding impertinences. At our time of life, to be alone sometimes is as needful as sleep. It is the freshing sleep of the day. The growing infirmities of age manifest themselves in nothing more strongly, than in an inveterate dislike of interruption. While youth was, we had vast reversions in time future; we are reduced to a present pittance, and obliged to economise in that article. We bleed away our moments now as hardly as our

ducats. We cannot bear to have our thin wardrobe eaten and fretted into by moths. We are will-
ing to barter our good time with a friend, who gives
us in exchange his own. Herein is the distinction
between the genuine guest and the visitant. This
latter takes your good time, and gives you his bad in
exchange. The guest is domestic to you as your
good cat, or household bird; the visitant is your fly,
that flaps in at your window, and out again, leaving
nothing but a sense of disturbance, and victuals
spoiled.

— LAMB: *Popular Fallacies.*

This passage is full of comparisons, which
exemplify the fertile imagination of Lamb.
To what is the shortness of his time compared? What is a guest and a visitant like?
" We object to interruptions because the old
have little time and visitants disturb," is the
topic.

SUBJECTS

Imagine comparisons for:
The reading of good and of bad books.
Listening to a good and to a poor speaker.
We are delighted to travel on sea rather
than on land.
The people's idea of the drama and of
the picture play.
Our preference of one profession or trade
over another.

VIII.   EXPAND COMPARISONS

If a comparison is extended by an endeavor to establish many points of resemblance, it will usually be forced and fanciful or even ludicrous (Cf. Chap. XIV). Note this passage from Richardson quoted in the *King's English:*

> Tost to and fro by the high winds of passionate control, I behold the desired port, the single state, into which I fain would steer; but am kept off by the foaming billows of a brother's and a sister's envy, and by the raging winds of a supposed invaded authority; while I see in Lovelace, the rocks on the one hand, and in Solmes, the sands on the other; and tremble, lest I should split upon the former or strike upon the latter! But you, my better pilot, . . .

If, however, the single point of comparison becomes clearer and more effective or if the object with which the comparison is made receives vivid presentation, then the advantages are many. A careful taste is needed. The following passage from Arnold may serve as an example where an incident of history interestingly told is made the basis for comparison. Only one point of resemblance is noted. Had Arnold spoken of a crusading middle-class, with infant limbs scaling mountain difficulties, the comparison would be far-fetched and absurd.

In the crusade of Peter the Hermit, where the hosts that marched were not filled after the usual composition of armies, but contained along with the fighters whole families of people,— old men, women, and children,— swept by the universal torrent of enthusiasm toward the Holy Land, the marches, as might have been expected, were tedious and painful. Long before Asia was reached, long before even Europe was half traversed, the little children in that travelling multitude began to fancy, with a natural impatience, that their journey must surely be drawing to an end; and every evening, as they came in sight of some town which was the destination of that day's march, they cried out eagerly to those who were with them: "Is this Jerusalem?" No, poor children, not this town, nor the next nor yet the next, is Jerusalem; Jerusalem is far off, and it needs time, and strength, and much endurance to reach it. Seas and mountains, labor and peril, hunger and thirst, disease and death, are between Jerusalem and you.

So, when one marks the ferment and stir of life in the middle class at this moment, and sees this class impelled to take possession of the world, and to assert itself and its own actual spirit absolutely, one is disposed to exclaim to it: "Jerusalem is not yet. Your present spirit is not Jerusalem, is not the goal you have to reach, the place you may be satisfied with."

— ARNOLD: *A French Eton.*

I.

Boston has five or six trains of railroads,— one
to the Old Colony, one to Providence, one to Wor-
cester, one to Lowell, one to Fitchburg, one to the
eastern counties. All of them run locomotives
where they wish to. Suppose that, on the Fitchburg Railroad, one locomotive, for a year, never got
farther than Groton,— what do you think the Direc-
tors of that road would do? Would they take up
the rails beyond Groton, or would they turn out the
engineer? There is a law of the Commonwealth
of Massachusetts, thoroughly executed in every
county but ours; and here the men appointed to
execute it, not only do not want to, but you cannot
expect them to. They were elected not to execute
it, and they say they can't execute it. Shall we take
up the rails, or change the engineer? — which?

— PHILLIPS: *Metropolitan Police.*

"A train requires a good engineer to run
it; a law in the same way requires a good officer to enforce it." The comparison is ex-
panded and made local for Phillips' hearers,
and then is applied.

SUBJECTS

*Imagine yourself speaking to a definite au-
dience and expand with apt details these comparisons:*

Forming a character is like minting coin.
Sentry duty is the acid test of a soldier's courage.

Building a library is building a lighthouse.

Wendell Phillips during life was like a woodman "hewing toward the light."— O'REILLY.

In school you make timepieces for life.

"The man who has nothing to boast of but ancestors is like a potato — his good is underground."

2.

Neither do I acknowledge, sir, the right of Plymouth to the whole rock. No, the rock underlies all America; it only crops out here. (Cheers.) It has cropped out a great many times in our history. You may recognize it always. Old Putnam stood upon it at Bunker Hill, when he said to the Yankee boys, "Don't fire till you see the whites of their eyes." Ingraham had it for ballast when he put his little sloop between two Austrian frigates, and threatened to blow them out of the water, if they did not respect the broad eagle of the United States, in the case of Koszta. Jefferson had it for a writing-desk when he drafted the Declaration of Independence and the "Statute of Religious Liberty" for Virginia. Lovejoy rested his musket upon it when they would not let him print at Alton, and he said "Death or free speech!" I recognized the clink of it to-day, when the apostle of the "Higher Law" came to lay his garland of everlasting — none a better right than he — upon the monument of the Pilgrims. (Enthusiastic cheering.) He says he is not a descendant of the Pilgrims. That is a mistake. There is a pedigree of the body and a pedigree of the mind. (Applause.)

He knows so much about the *Mayflower* that, as
they say in the West, I know he was " thar "
(Laughter and applause).   Ay, sir, the rock cropped
out again.   Garrison had it for an imposing-stone
when he looked in the faces of seventeen millions of
angry men and printed his sublime pledge, " I will
not retreat a single inch, and I will be heard."
(Great cheering.)

— WENDELL PHILLIPS: *The Pilgrims.*

The courageous upholding of principles is
compared to the Plymouth Rock, which crops
out in history in many instances.   The ex-
tending of a comparison in this way is likely
to become fanciful and even ludicrous.
Here the taste and enthusiasm of the speaker
keeps the passage from descending too far,
although he is not averse to a touch of
humor.

SUBJECTS

Expand the comparisons:

The Statute of Liberty has been erected everywhere in our country.

The American flag floats patriotically wherever a
citizen observes the laws.

The Bible has been the light of the world.

The Cross of Calvary has been the stay of martyrs.

Here once the embattled farmers stood
And fired the shot heard round the world.

— EMERSON: *Hymn at Concord.*

3.

Coming to Shelley's poetry, we peep over the wild
mask of revolutionary metaphysics, and we see the
winsome face of the child. Perhaps none of his
poems is more purely and typically Shelleian than
The Cloud and it is interesting to note how essentially it springs from the faculty of make-believe.
The same thing is conspicuous, though less purely
conspicuous, throughout his singing; it is the child's
faculty of make-believe raised to the nth power.
He is still at play save only that his play is such as
manhood stops to watch and his playthings are
those which the gods give their children. The universe is his box of toys. He dabbles his fingers in
the day-fall. He is gold-dusty with tumbling
amidst the stars. He makes bright mischief with
the moon. The meteors muzzle their noses in his
hand. He teases into growling the kenneled thunder, and laughs at the shaking of its fiery chain.
He dances in and out of the gates of heaven; its
floor is littered with his broken fancies. He runs
wild over the fields of ether. He chases the falling
world. He gets between the feet of the horses of
the sun. He stands in the lap of patient nature,
and twines her loosened tresses after a hundred wil-
ful fashions to see how she will look nicest in his
song.

— THOMPSON: *Shelley.*

A successful expanding of a comparison,
but it is admitted by the writer to be fanciful
and playful. The handling of the topic and

its diction are akin to the poetical, fitly so, where a poet is praising a poet. In fact Thompson (*Anthem to the Earth*) has the close of this paragraph in his poetry with a few changes.

SUBJECTS

Expand with less ornateness:

The sunbeam is the earth's painter.
Winter puts the world to sleep.
Spring is the land's awakener.
" Life is a warfare."

SYNOPSIS OF CONTENTS

CHAPTER I. THE TIRESOME SPEAKER

New wrappers for old thoughts. The conventional is tiresome. By triteness words become colorless signs. Illustrations not made actual. What is undignified. To be dignified and tiresome avoid the specific. Dramatic pictures. Imagination, the natural enemy of tiresomeness.........….*Page* 3

CHAPTER II. INTEREST FROM DIRECTNESS

Speech is talked directly to some one. Tiresome sermons are essays for anyone. Looking forward to publication. Effect of a definite audience in panegyrics and in debates. Directness in Demosthenes and Cicero, Burke and Fox. A modern instance. Style of a letter, result of directness. Epistles of St. Paul, models of directness. Sermons animated; essays quiet. Figures of speech, differences between spoken and written language. St. Paul exemplifies striking figures. Energy of St. Paul due to figures. Lively directness strange to eyes, not to ears. Directness from emotion, which is chilled in print.

313

St. Paul, model of emotional directness. Second Epistle to the Corinthians....*Page* 19

CHAPTER III.   THE ART OF ELOQUENCE AND
THE SCIENCE OF THEOLOGY

Changing theology into eloquence. Modifying the form of truth for clearness, interest and force. Eloquence untechnical; technical terms useful, but obscure to the many. Energy and time needed to transmute science to art. Pardow realizing God's personality. Art concrete: science abstract. Philosophical commentary of imaginative Scripture. Religious terminology and the Bible original. Science is calm; art emotional. Science hastens to new truth: art pauses on good or evil, and searches the imagination to embody truth.

Page 37

CHAPTER IV.   THE IMAGINATION OF THE
SPEAKER

Earnest but insulated. Speaker must strive to reach all. Earnestness not enough. Quintilian's famous formula and its meaning. Necessity of the imagination. Active and passive imagination. Development of imagination by fiction and by poetry. Hebrew poetry superior to Greek and Latin for this purpose. Hebrew imagination emancipated by Genesis. Coign of vantage over creation; view-point of Creator; mastery of universe; might of God, weakness of man. Archimedes lever for the imagination. Speakers not insulated: Benson, Vaughan. Imaginative fictions ....*Page* 53

CHAPTER V. INTEREST FROM EMOTIONS

Reason is dry; emotion pleasant. Rhetorical neglect of emotion. Philosophy of emotions disputed. Emotion from beauty. Emotion from good or evil. Difference between these emotions. Beauty static; good kinetic. Appetitive emotion necessary for practical application; for probable conclusions. Voluntary action in both cases. Place of beauty in oratory. Three graces of eloquence: truth, beauty, goodness ....*Page* 73

CHAPTER VI. MEMORY AS A TEST OF INTEREST

The good of forgotten sermons. A memory experiment on a newspaper reporter, a defective medium in profession and style. Remembrance by reiteration; by novel presentation, in stories, in historical facts, in similes, and in epigrams. Remembrance by personality and by sincere emotion. Actuality, the chief cause of remembrance. How to write a sermon that will stick.
Page 87

CHAPTER VII. NEWMAN AND THE
ACADEMIC STYLE

Newman's Catholic sermons. Definiteness
and popularity. *The Second Spring* definite, but not telling its subject soon
enough. Newman like Cicero, in musical prose, varied and smooth and copious
but tending to diffuseness in exposition.
Newman not romantic but classical. Not
like Cicero in arrangement of whole sermon, which has two parts, without the
classic exordium. Internal structure has
long exposition followed by an impassioned close, Hebraic in nature. *Second
Spring* changed to classic form. Newman
academic. Excellent and less good qualities. *Sermon Notes* show same academic
traits in poetical comparison, subtle analogies, learned allusions, early and lengthy
discussion of the general topic.......*Page* 99

CHAPTER VIII. PARDOW AND THE POPULAR
STYLE

His vocation to preaching. Sees comparisons
in everything about him. Vocabulary not
vulgar, not literary. Distinct talker.
Ever in touch with his audience and a
popularizer. Imaginative in dramatic
exposition, in developing comparisons, in
caricaturing and satirizing. Homiletic in
build of sermons; with unity of im-

pression rather than unity of expression. The style was the man in delivery. Taught by *Spiritual Exercises*. Personality and higher qualities .... *Page* 123

CHAPTER IX. INTEREST FROM ANTAGONISM

Best speech a duel. Demosthenes and Aeschines. Cicero in refutations. Value of antagonist illustrated in the speeches of Bryan, a debater. Inferior to Phillips, a fierce antagonist. Speeches without opponent, valedictory, complimentary. Specific effects of rivalry on the style. Illustrative instances. The Chicago Convention Speech. Contrasts, echoes, dilemma, retorts. Better but more familiar illustrations in more famous orators .... *Page* 143

CHAPTER X. MACAULAY AND "JOURNALESE"

Literature eager for immortality. Journalism content with a brief existence. Winning a distracted reader. Interest of news and of other journalistic writings. "Journalese." Its methods: never be dull, omit introductions and all conjunctions. Its father, Macaulay; by assertiveness, epigrams, balance, omission of pronouns. Examples of Macaulay's comparisons. His secret: omit all qualifications. Henry James and Mr. Saintsbury. Some inconveniences; exaggeration, inconsistencies .... *Page* 155

CHAPTER XI. LITERARY AGILITY

Cleverness demands rapidity. Manipulating
  contrasts and mastering contradictories:
  Sophists, Cicero, Plutarch, Abelard,
  Macaulay. Reducing everything to a
  common denominator: Dickens and Douglas. Harmonizing contradictories: Chesterton. Excess of plausibility .....*Page* 165

CHAPTER XII. TABB AND FANCY

Not fanciful as a rule, in language or meter.
  The suggestiveness of imaginative poetry
  — Homer, Shakespeare, T e n n y s o n.
  Some examples in Tabb. The momentary
  appeal of poetry of fancy. The elabora-
  tion of comparisons. Herrick, Wordsworth and Tabb. Religious poetry *Page* 175

CHAPTER XIII. POETRY AND INTEREST

All arts have audiences to hold and attract.
  The poet, once teacher of the people, must
  still be popular. Greek epic, lyric, drama,
  pastoral, began with the people, became
  conventional and retired to the closet.
  Modern poetry chafes at the conventional
  — Wordsworth, Browning, Patmore,
  Whitman, Kipling. Poetry teaches truth
  of things, ontological truths in description, truth of statements, logical truth, and
  finally moral truth. All poets teach, not
  by reasoning but by revelation ....*Page* 191

CHAPTER XIV. NOVELTY OR ECCENTRICITY

Vagaries in the search for interest. Language
    to be a transparent medium, not an end
    in itself.   In all arts no obtruding of the
    medium: music, painting, sculpture. Ro-
    din's Hand of God. Originality not in
    the medium. Bottom's actors rivalled
    by musicians and painters. Interest not
    in straining the medium on its material or
    formal side.   Imitative effects in language:
    Southey, Newman. Fancifulness in odd
    comparisons or extended comparisons. A
    new definition of fancy ....*Page* 199

CHAPTER XV. THE NEED OF IMAGINATION

Interest differs from amusement.   Interest may
    come from extrinsic sources or from the
    subject matter. Interest from language
    in question here. Clearness, force, inter-
    est. Other terms for the idea. Chief
    source of interest in the imagination.
    Testimony of Mullois and Potter. Im-
    agination, the storehouse of sense percep-
    tions. Interest in the specific, concrete,
    local; in detail. Translation of an im-
    aginative passage into the abstract and gen-
    eral. Comparison of original. Aquinas,
    the philosopher, and Newman, imagina-
    tive writer. Other sources of interest
    within the sphere of the imagination *Page* 215

CHAPTER XVI. DEVELOPING THE IMAGINATION

All past sights, sounds, etc., submerged in the
imagination. Reflection, first means, recalls past visions. Metaphors revived by
reflection. Realization, a second means,
making words reveal their pictures.
Translating by things. Visualizing helps
realization and imagination. Reading, a
third means. Advantages of poetry.
Contrast of fiction and poetry. How to
read with the imagination. Not insincerity or untruth. Lowell's statement *Page* 225

CHAPTER XVII. IS ESTHETIC EMOTION A
SPINAL THRILL?

History of terms, imagination and fancy:
Wordsworth, Coleridge, Hunt, Ruskin.
Meaning ascribed to these terms by these
authors. The current term for art and
literature is emotion, a vague term. Winchester refuses to define it. Consequent
inconsistencies. The spinal thrill, latest
test of poetry. Keble and Newman.
Balfour's distinction of appetitive and
esthetic emotions. Same as that of
Aquinas and of scholastic philosophy.
Specific differences between two kinds of
emotions. Appetitive emotions may be
the subject matter of the arts, or constitute the specific difference between
types of poetry. The generic note of art

according to Aristotle is "imitation" or dramatization. Proper meaning of imagination and emotion ....*Page* 237

CHAPTER XVIII. ORIGINALITY BY IMITATION

Demand for originality. Originality in the form; is natural, individual, creative yet borrowed, distinctive. Excesses in originality. Like energy in transformation. Imitation necessary. Source of ideas. Transmuting ideas into original thought. Personal thought; warming of imagination. Observing one's own thought. Admiring on principle. Imitating and copying. Coleridge's epigram from Reynolds' teaching ....*Page* 251

CHAPTER XIX. EXERCISES FOR THE IMAGINATION

Limit the topic. Define a statement. Dwell on the pictures of poetry. Put the concrete for the abstract. Put the particular for the general. Put a significant part for the whole. Learn to make comparisons. Expand comparisons ....*Page* 267

14 DAY USE

RETURN TO DESK FROM WHICH BORROWED

LOAN DEPT.

This book is due on the last date stamped below, or
on the date to which renewed.
Renewed books are subject to immediate recall.

26

REC'D LD

JUL 24 1966

RETD LD

DEC 16 1960

JAN

MAY 5 1967 7 7

MAY 2 6 67 -10 AM

REC'D LD

LD 21A–50m-8,'57
(C8481s10)476B

General Library
University of California
Berkeley

JAN 2 1929

Lightning Source UK Ltd.
Milton Keynes UK
UKHW021837080519
342351UK00003B/49/P